SARAH E. PAUL
AND DANIEL L. KURTZ

MANAGING CONFLICTS OF INTEREST THIRD EDITION

THE BOARD'S GUIDE TO UNBIASED DECISION MAKING

BOARDSOURCE®

Library of Congress Cataloging-in-Publication Data

Kurtz, Daniel L.
  Managing conflicts of interest : the board's guide to unbiased decision making /
Sarah E. Paul and Daniel L. Kurtz. -- Third edition.
    page cm.

Includes bibliographical references.
ISBN 1-58686-133-6
1. Nonprofit organizations--United States--Management. 2. Conflict of
interests--United States. I. Paul, Sarah E. (Sarah Elizabeth), 1964- II. BoardSource
(Organization) III. Title.
  HD62.6.K87 2013
  658.4'22--dc23

                2012047461

© 2013 BoardSource.
First Printing, January 2013
  ISBN 1-58686-133-6

Published by BoardSource
750 9th Street, NW, Suite 650
Washington, DC 20001

BOARDSOURCE®
Building Effective Nonprofit Boards

BoardSource is dedicated to advancing the public good by building exceptional nonprofit boards and inspiring board service.

BoardSource was established in 1988 by the Association of Governing Boards of Universities and Colleges (AGB) and Independent Sector (IS). Prior to this, in the early 1980s, the two organizations had conducted a survey and found that although 30 percent of respondents believed they were doing a good job of board education and training, the rest of the respondents reported little, if any, activity in strengthening governance. As a result, AGB and IS proposed the creation of a new organization whose mission would be to increase the effectiveness of nonprofit boards.

With a lead grant from the Kellogg Foundation and funding from five other donors, BoardSource opened its doors in 1988 as the National Center for Nonprofit Boards with a staff of three and an operating budget of $385,000. On January 1, 2002, BoardSource took on its new name and identity. These changes were the culmination of an extensive process of understanding how we were perceived, what our audiences wanted, and how we could best meet the needs of nonprofit organizations.

Today, BoardSource is the premier voice of nonprofit governance. Its highly acclaimed products, programs, and services mobilize boards so that organizations fulfill their missions, achieve their goals, increase their impact, and extend their influence. BoardSource is a 501(c)(3) organization.

BoardSource provides

- resources to nonprofit leaders through workshops, training, and an extensive Web site (www.boardsource.org)

- governance consultants who work directly with nonprofit leaders to design specialized solutions to meet an organization's needs

- the world's largest, most comprehensive selection of material on nonprofit governance, including a large selection of books and toolkits

- an annual conference that brings together approximately 900 governance experts, board members, and chief executives and senior staff from around the world

For more information, please visit our Web site at www.boardsource.org, e-mail us at mail@boardsource.org, or call us at 800-883-6262.

Essential Resources from BoardSource

THE GOVERNANCE SERIES

Ten Basic Responsibilities of Nonprofit Boards, Second Edition

Legal Responsibilities of Nonprofit Boards, Second Edition

Financial Responsibilities of Nonprofit Boards, Second Edition

Fundraising Responsibilities of Nonprofit Boards, Second Edition

The Nonprofit Board's Role in Mission, Planning, and Evaluation, Second Edition

Structures and Practices of Nonprofit Boards, Second Edition

THE COMMITTEE SERIES

Transforming Board Structure: Strategies for Committees and Task Forces

Governance Committee

Executive Committee

Financial Committees

Development Committee

Advisory Councils

OTHER PUBLICATIONS

Better Bylaws: Creating Effective Rules for Your Nonprofit Board, Second Edition

Board Fundamentals: Understanding Roles in Nonprofit Governance, Second Edition

Building the Governance Partnership: The Chief Executive's Guide to Getting the Best from the Board, Second Edition

Chief Executive Succession Planning: Essential Guidance for Boards and CEOs, Second Edition

Chief Executive Transitions: How to Hire and Support a Nonprofit CEO

Culture of Inquiry: Healthy Debate in the Boardroom

Driving Strategic Planning: A Nonprofit Executive's Guide, Second Edition

Fearless Fundraising for Nonprofit Boards, Second Edition

Generate Buzz: Strategic Communication for Nonprofit Boards, Second Edition

Governance as Leadership: Reframing the Work of Nonprofit Boards

Govern Green: Driving Your Organization's Commitment to Sustainability

Govern More, Manage Less: Harnessing the Power of Your Nonprofit Board, Second Edition

Meeting, and Exceeding Expectations: A Guide to Successful Nonprofit Board Meetings, Second Edition

Moving Beyond Founder's Syndrome to Nonprofit Success

Navigating the Organizational Lifecycle: A Capacity-Building Guide for Nonprofit Leaders

Nonprofit Executive Compensation: Planning, Performance, and Pay, Second Edition

Taming the Troublesome Board Member

Ten Basic Responsibilities of Nonprofit Boards: The Companion Workbook

The Board Building Cycle: Nine Steps to Finding, Recruiting, and Engaging Nonprofit Board Members, Second Edition

The Board Chair Handbook, Third Edition

The Business Professional's Guide to Nonprofit Board Service: Leveraging Your Talents for the Social Sector, Second Edition

The Handbook of Nonprofit Governance

The Nonprofit Board Answer Book: A Practical Guide for Board Members and Chief Executives, Third Edition

The Nonprofit Chief Executive's Ten Basic Responsibilities, Second Edition

The Nonprofit Dashboard: Using Metrics to Drive Mission Success, Second Edition

The Nonprofit Policy Sampler, Second Edition

The Source: Twelve Principles of Governance That Power Exceptional Boards

Trouble at the Top: The Nonprofit Board's Guide to Managing an Imperfect Chief Executive

Understanding Nonprofit Financial Statements, Third Edition

Who's Minding the Money? An Investment Guide for Nonprofit Board Members, Second Edition

Wrestling with Board Dilemmas: Case Studies for Nonprofit Leaders

DVDs

Meeting the Challenge: An Orientation to Nonprofit Board Service
Speaking of Money: A Guide to Fundraising for Nonprofit Board Members

ONLINE ASSESSMENTS

Board Self-Assessment

Assessment of the Chief Executive

Executive Search — Needs Assessment

For up-to-date information and prices on publications, assessments, consulting, training, and membership, please call BoardSource at 800-883-6262 or visit our Web site at www.boardsource.org. For consulting services, please e-mail us at consulting@boardsource.org or call 877-892-6293.

CONTENTS

INTRODUCTION. 1
   What Is a Conflict of Interest?. 1
   Overview 2

CHAPTER 1. CONTINUING SCRUTINY OF NONPROFIT ORGANIZATIONS 5
   IRS Application for Recognition of Tax Exemption 5
   IRS Governance Check Sheet. 6
   IRS Form 990. 7
   Scrutiny of Nonprofit Organizations by States and Funders. 8

CHAPTER 2. HOW CONFLICTS OF INTEREST ARISE. 11
   Legal Duties of Board Members. 12
   Situations That Give Rise to Conflicts of Interest. 13
      Financial Conflict. 13
      Loyalty to More Than One Nonprofit Organization 18
      Corporate Opportunity 20
      Conflicting Roles and Relationships 20
   The Conflict-of-Interest Continuum 22
      Case Studies. 23

CHAPTER 3. CONFLICTS OF INTEREST AND THE LAW 25
   State Laws 25
   Federal Tax Law. 26
      Private Inurement 26
      Private Benefit 27
      Intermediate Sanctions Rules 28
      Excess Benefit Transactions. 29
      Penalties for Excess Benefit Transactions 30
      Rebuttable Presumption of Reasonableness 31
      Excess Benefit Transactions and Maintenance of
      Tax-Exempt Status. 32
      Excess Benefit Transaction Rules Applicable to
      Supporting Organizations and Donor Advised Funds. 33
      Self-Dealing Rules Applicable to Private Foundations 34
   Other Laws. 36

CHAPTER 4. THE CONFLICT-OF-INTEREST POLICY: ADDRESSING CONFLICTS BEFORE PROBLEMS ARISE 37
Diversity on the Board: An Essential Component 37
Creating the Policy. 38
   Case Study: The Holyoke Medical Center..................... 40
   Who Should Be Covered by the Policy? 41
   To Whom Are Conflicting Interests Reported?................ 42
Components of the Conflict-of-Interest Policy 43
   Statement of Purpose and Duties of Officers and Directors 43
   Direct or Indirect Financial, Competing, or Other Material Interest 44
   What Happens When a Direct or Indirect Financial, Competing, or Other Material Interest Is Reported? 47
   Co-Investment Interest 49
   Failure to Disclose...................................... 49
The Disclosure Statement 50
Special Considerations: Foundations. 51
Serving a Broad Purpose 52

CHAPTER 5. ADDRESSING CONFLICTS OF INTEREST AFTER PROBLEMS ARISE 55
Establishing a Procedure for Responding 55
   Discussion with the Conflicted Board Member................ 56
   What Should Be Done after the Discussion?.................. 56
   Handling a Problem That Arises during a Board Meeting....... 57
   Discovery of Failure to Disclose 57

CHAPTER 6. CONFLICTS OF INTEREST AND ETHICAL CONSIDERATIONS 59
Organizational Code of Ethics................................ 59
   Developing a Written Policy 60
Creating a Culture of Integrity 60

CHAPTER 7. WHISTLEBLOWER POLICY 63
Contents of the Policy 64

CONCLUSION 67

APPENDIX 1. Q&AS 69

APPENDIX 2. IRS FORM 1023 REQUIREMENTS, INSTRUCTIONS, AND SAMPLE IRS CONFLICT-OF-INTEREST POLICY 73

APPENDIX 3. SAMPLE CONFLICT-OF-INTEREST POLICY 79

APPENDIX 4. SAMPLE CONFLICT-OF-INTEREST DISCLOSURE STATEMENT........ 85

APPENDIX 5. SAMPLE POLICY FOR THE PROMOTION OF ETHICAL CONDUCT 87

APPENDIX 6. SAMPLE WHISTLEBLOWER POLICY 89

GLOSSARY 93

SUGGESTED RESOURCES 99

ABOUT THE AUTHORS 101

INTRODUCTION

Individuals who volunteer to serve on nonprofit boards tend to be actively engaged in their communities and have a myriad of professional, personal, and community relationships. Many serve on more than one nonprofit board at a time. The nonprofit sector depends on the spirit of volunteerism displayed by these engaged and capable individuals. However, these board members can also face challenges in carrying out their board responsibilities precisely because of the number and breadth of the associations and connections they have. Making unbiased, independent decisions on behalf of the organization can be difficult when a colleague, a friend, a family member, another organization, or a business relationship may be affected by or benefit from those decisions. The more connected a board member is, the more likely it is that such intertwining circumstances will arise, creating potential and sometimes problematic conflicts of interest.

This book seeks to demystify many of the legal rules relating to conflicts of interest that are applicable to nonprofit board members and executive staff, giving current and prospective board members the knowledge they need to serve with confidence. Because there are many legal definitions and nuances involved, this text seeks to create both a common understanding of conflicts of interest and a common vocabulary with which to discuss conflict issues.

The best approach to managing conflicts of interest may vary from one nonprofit organization to another, but all nonprofits share the fundamental need for impartial decision making. When making decisions, board members must set aside personal agendas and put the interests of the organization above all else. Conflicting interests will always be a key issue for nonprofit organizations, which require the care and attention of board members who are active and engaged.

WHAT IS A CONFLICT OF INTEREST?

A conflict of interest exists when a board member, officer, or management employee has a personal interest that is in conflict with the interests of the organization, such that he or she may be influenced by this personal interest when making a decision for the organization. Conflicting interests may include both financial and nonfinancial concerns, although the law is most often concerned with and focused on financial interests. While the term conflict of interest has taken on a negative connotation, only some of the many different types of conflicts of interest may actually be harmful to an organization. How an organization manages conflicts of interest and ensures open and honest deliberation affects all aspects of its operations and is critical to avoiding legal problems and public scandals, making good decisions, and remaining focused on the organization's mission.

The key for nonprofit boards is not to try to avoid all possible conflict-of-interest situations, which would be impossible; rather, boards need to identify and follow a process for handling them effectively. There is no single solution to addressing conflicts that will best suit every nonprofit organization. It is essential to keep in mind the importance of disinterested decision making so that all board members can aid their organizations in determining how best to address conflict concerns, which helps to protect them and the organizations they serve. As board members and chief executives gain a greater understanding of the legal and organizational concerns surrounding conflicting interests, they will be able to help their organizations distinguish between situations in which conflicting interests can be beneficial to the organization and situations where a board member may be using his or her role to gain a personal advantage. Developing this ability enables board members to concentrate more on the challenges and psychic rewards that accompany nonprofit service.

The issue of conflicts of interest also relates to the more general subject of ethical conduct. Many organizations seek not simply to comply with legal regulations — which is required — but also to encourage the highest standards of behavior by its board and staff. This is not purely a concern for high-mindedness; donors and volunteers of nonprofit organizations trust organizations to be good stewards of their resources and to uphold rigorous standards of conduct and personal integrity.

OVERVIEW

The first chapter of this book describes the continuing scrutiny of nonprofit organizations by the Internal Revenue Service (IRS) and state attorneys general. The second chapter details the legal duties of board members, describes how conflicts of interest may arise, and explains that not all conflicts of interest are illegal or unacceptable. To help board members think through potential conflicts of interest, it acknowledges the difficulty of defining conflicts by illustrating them in terms of a continuum, with unacceptable (illegal) conflicts at one end and inconsequential conflicts at the other, with a range of situations in between.

The third chapter addresses legal considerations in detail, aiming to clarify the legal concepts and terms, and give nonprofit board members the knowledge they need to act in accordance with state and federal law. This chapter includes a discussion of the IRS intermediate sanctions rules applicable to public charities as well as the stricter self-dealing rules that private foundations must follow. The material is intended as a basic guide and will also help board members recognize when they may need the advice of a legal professional.

Chapters 4 and 5 outline the steps a nonprofit board should take to ensure that it is prepared to handle conflicts of interest proactively and constructively. Chapter 4 discusses the conflict-of-interest policy and board member disclosure statement in detail. Chapter 5 provides guidelines for responding to conflicts of interest that have already become problematic.

Chapter 6 looks at the broader ethical context, seeking to provide guidance for board members as they consider the ramifications of their actions in terms of public perception and personal integrity, and discusses the increasing interest in having an organizational code of ethics.

Chapter 7 describes the requirement in the Sarbanes-Oxley Act that nonprofit organizations provide protection for whistleblowers and sets out some considerations when preparing a whistleblower policy.

The appendices include Q&As and sample policies and forms. A glossary of key terms follows the appendices.

CHAPTER 1

Continuing Scrutiny of Nonprofit Organizations

The need for board members to understand the legal landscape surrounding conflicts of interest, as well as public perceptions in this regard, is particularly important given the increased scrutiny of nonprofits by government regulators and by the public.

The IRS, state attorneys general, Congress, and the media are continuing to focus on the nonprofit sector and the extent to which boards fulfill their oversight responsibilities. The Taxpayer Bill of Rights 2 introduced intermediate sanctions for excess benefit transactions (see Chapter 3), and regulations were finalized in 2002.

IRS APPLICATION FOR RECOGNITION OF TAX EXEMPTION

Any new nonprofit organization seeking Federal tax exemption must address at the outset how it will manage conflicts of interest. The June 2006 version of the IRS Application for Recognition of Exemption Under Section 501(c)(3) of the Internal Revenue Code (the Form 1023), includes extensive questions on conflicts of interest.[1] A sample conflict-of-interest policy is included with the Form, and each organization filing the Form must state whether it has adopted a conflict-of-interest policy consistent with the sample policy. If the organization has adopted a similar policy, it is asked to include a copy with its application and to explain how it was adopted (such as by resolution of the board). If no such policy is in place, the organization must describe what procedures will be followed to ensure that conflicts of interest will be managed wisely. The Form states that, although a conflict-of-interest policy is recommended, it is not required in order to obtain exemption. The instructions do provide, however, that "by adopting the sample policy or similar policy, you will be choosing to put in place procedures that will help you avoid the possibility that those in positions of authority over you may receive an inappropriate benefit."[2] (A copy of the IRS policy that accompanies the Form 1023 is included in Appendix 2.)

---

[1]   I.R.S. Form 1023, *Application for Recognition of Exemption Under Section 501(c)(3) of the Internal Revenue Code* (2006), available at http://www.irs.gov/pub/irs-pdf/f1023.pdf.

[2]   I.R.S. Instructions to Form 1023, *Application for Recognition of Exemption Under Section 501(c)(3) of the Internal Revenue Code*, 9 (2006), available at http://www.irs.gov/pub/irs-pdf/i1023.pdf.

The Form also asks specific questions about potential conflict-of-interest transactions. Each organization must state whether it has any business relationship with any of its officers, directors, or trustees, and whether any of the organization's officers, directors, or trustees are related to any of the organization's highest compensated employees or independent contractors through family or business relationships. The Form also requires information about the extent to which individuals running the organization are independent of one another. The question in that regard is whether any of the organization's officers, directors, or trustees are related to each other through any family or business relationship.

IRS GOVERNANCE CHECK SHEET

The IRS has repeatedly expressed its view that good governance of 501(c)(3) public charities and tax compliance go hand in hand. Questions on governance on the revised Form 990 (Annual Information Return), discussed below, reflect the IRS' increased interest in nonprofit governance.[3] In addition, in 2009, the IRS created a Governance Check Sheet to be used by revenue agents during examinations of 501(c)(3) public charities to gather information on organizations' governance practices and internal controls.[4] The Governance Check Sheet includes a section on conflicts of interest that asks whether the organization has a written conflict-of-interest policy and if so, whether it addresses recusals; whether the policy requires written disclosure of conflicts of interest; and if during the organization's examination year any conflict of interest was disclosed, whether the organization's conflict-of-interest policy was adhered to.

Based on these questions, it is clear that having a conflict-of-interest policy that sits on a shelf is not sufficient. It must be a living document used by the organization to regularly and actively manage conflicts of interest. This is evidenced also by inquiries that have been conducted in recent years by the Attorney General of the Commonwealth of Massachusetts as discussed in Chapter 4 in the detailed discussion of the conflict policy.

The Governance Check Sheet also asks whether any of the organization's board members have a family and/or business relationship with any other voting or non-voting board member, officer, director or trustee, or key employee. Here, as on the IRS Form 1023, the IRS is looking for relationships that might cause a board member to make a decision for the organization based on the board member's personal interest rather than on his or her judgment as to what would be best for the organization.

---

[3]   I.R.S. Form 990, *Return of Organization Exempt from Income Tax* (2011), available at http://www.irs.gov/pub/irs-pdf/f990.pdf.

[4]   I.R.S. Form 14114, *Governance Check Sheet* (2009), available at http://www.irs.gov/pub/irs-tege/governance_check_sheet.pdf.

IRS FORM 990

Every organization that files the Form 990 (Annual Information Return) must state whether it has a written conflict-of-interest policy.[5] If the organization does have a conflict policy, the organization must answer whether officers, directors or trustees, and key employees are required to disclose annually interests that could give rise to conflicts and whether the organization regularly and consistently monitors and enforces compliance with the policy. If so, the organization is required to describe its means of monitoring and enforcing the conflicts policy. The description should include an explanation of which persons are covered under the policy and who at the organization is responsible for determining whether a conflict exists. The organization also should explain any restrictions imposed on persons with a conflict, such as prohibiting them from participating in the governing body's deliberations and decisions on the transactions.

Although all organizations should have a conflict policy in place, it is important to remember that both the IRS and state attorneys general will require that the organization closely follow the process it has created for managing conflicts. Accordingly, a policy should not be adopted without a process for educating officers and directors about the policy and for obtaining and reviewing the information the organization needs to monitor conflicts of interest.

The IRS Form 990 also now includes an entire schedule (Schedule L) titled "Transactions with Interested Persons."[6] Schedule L requires reporting of the following four different transactions with interested persons: (i) excess benefit transactions, (ii) loans to and/or from interested persons, (iii) grants or assistance benefiting interested persons, and (iv) business transactions involving interested persons. Reporting is made complicated by the fact that different definitions of "interested persons" and different reporting thresholds apply to the different transactions.

An organization also must disclose on the Form 990 whether any officer, director, trustee, or key employee has a family or business relationship with any other officer, director or trustee, or employee.

Because responses to these questions on the Form 990 require obtaining information from third parties, each organization must develop a means for gathering this information. The instructions to the Form 990 require that the organization make

---

[5]   The organization may answer yes to this question if the organization's board (or a committee of the board, if the board delegated authority to that committee to adopt the policy) adopted the conflict policy by the end of the tax year covered by the Form 990 being completed.

[6]   I.R.S. Form 990, *Return of Organization Exempt from Income Tax, Schedule L: Transactions with Interested Persons* (2011), available at http://www.irs.gov/pub/irs-pdf/f990sl.pdf.

reasonable efforts to obtain this information.[7] This may be done by distributing an annual questionnaire. Each organization should consider whether it wishes to time its distribution of such a questionnaire to coincide with distribution of its conflicts-of-interest disclosure form, which is discussed in detail in Chapter 4. Organizations also should be aware of whether any responses on the Form 990 implicate conflicts of interest under the terms of the organization's conflict-of-interest policy and, if so, how such conflicts were disclosed and how the conflict policy was monitored and enforced.

SCRUTINY OF NONPROFIT ORGANIZATIONS BY STATES AND FUNDERS

Funders and credit rating agencies nationwide also are looking with increasing attention at organizations' management, including the way they deal with conflicts and similar governance issues. California's adoption of the California Nonprofit Integrity Act of 2004, which took effect for 2005, was the first example of state legislation aimed at regulating the internal governance practices of nonprofit organizations. The main focus of the California Act is to increase the attorney general's oversight of charitable entities and commercial fundraisers in the state through increased disclosure and reporting requirements; the legislation also contains a few Sarbanes-Oxley–type provisions and also may be applied to nonprofits qualified to do business in California even if they are not incorporated in the state.

In May 2012, the New York State Attorney General recommended a bill that would amend New York law to require every New York charity to adopt a conflict-of-interest policy aimed at ensuring that directors, officers, key employees, and trustees act in the best interest of the entity that they are serving.[8] While this bill was not enacted during the 2012 Legislative Session, it is expected that the bill, or a modified version thereof, will be re-introduced during the 2013 Legislative Session. Although the existing bill does not mandate any specific form of policy, it provides that the policy must include, among other things

1. identification of the circumstances that constitute a conflict of interest

2. procedures for disclosing the conflict of interest

3. a requirement that the person with the conflict of interest

---

[7]   I.R.S. Form 990, *Instructions for Form 990, Return of Organization Exempt from Income Tax* (2011), available at http://www.irs.gov/pub/irs-pdf/i990.pdf.

[8]   S. 7431, 235th Sess. (N.Y. 2011).

(a) not be present at or participate in the deliberation or vote on the matter involving the conflict

(b) not influence such deliberation or vote

4. a requirement that the existence and resolution of the conflict be documented in the entity's records, including minutes of the meeting at which the matter involving the conflict was discussed or voted on

Under the bill, all directors and trustees new to an organization must complete a disclosure statement prior to being elected or appointed, and all directors and trustees must complete an annual disclosure statement. In addition, all entities required to be registered with the New York State Attorney General must submit a copy of its conflict-of-interest policy to the attorney general.

CHAPTER 2
How Conflicts of Interest Arise

There are many motives and situations that can cause a board member to have multiple loyalties. Conflicts can arise in any nonprofit organization, and not all board members will recognize them as conflicts or view them in the same way. Laws regulating conflicts of interest primarily address financial conflicts. However, varying allegiances, or even perceived opposing loyalties may be severely disruptive of board functioning and may need to be formally addressed. As discussed below, this is particularly true when an individual serves on the board of two nonprofits that are contemplating a transaction with each other or that simply have similar missions and operate in the same program space.

Think, for example, of a group of people at an organization who run a particular social services program and who decide that they wish to be independent, but the management of the organization is emotionally tied to the program and consider it to be one of the organization's jewels and central to the organization's future growth and success. Now consider the same situation if some of the organization's board members serve on the board of another entity that wishes to work with and support the social services program but only if it is operated independently. Those board members who serve on both boards clearly have conflicting interests, which are all the more challenging if one organization's financial future would be jeopardized if the program in question spins off. Although, in such cases, board members do not stand to gain a personal financial benefit, it may be difficult for them to understand the extent and nature of their fiduciary obligations.

Potentially more problematic are situations where a transaction of the organization will result in a personal financial benefit to an individual or an entity in which he or she has an ownership interest. Consider, for example, a scientific researcher who serves on a nonprofit organization's scientific review committee that is voting on whether to bestow a grant on the researcher's institution. This grant will fund research that he conducts or that is conducted by the department he chairs; since compensation at medical research institutions is often based on grants received, this could be of direct personal benefit to the researcher.

To begin to understand how best to approach these situations, let's consider the legal duties that board members owe to the organizations they serve.

LEGAL DUTIES OF BOARD MEMBERS

The responsibility of a board member to promote the interests of the organization that she or he serves is generally understood to entail three duties: the duty of care, the duty of loyalty, and the duty of obedience. Being mindful of these three duties and the potential legal ramifications of conflict-of-interest situations will help board members understand why a proactive approach to understanding and managing conflicts of interest is so important for their organization. These duties generally arise out of state law.

The key concept underlying state conflict statutes and state case law is that in their service on a nonprofit board, board members must make decisions that they believe are in the best interests of the organization — not decisions that further their own interests or the interests of a third party. This is known as the duty of loyalty. The duty of loyalty also requires that directors and officers not use their positions in the organization, or knowledge acquired through their association with the organization, to advance a personal agenda at the organization's expense. Understanding the duty of loyalty is critical to the evaluation of conflict-of-interest situations. For example, if a board member works as an investment manager and also serves on an organization's investment committee, may he recommend that the organization invest with his company? If so, under what circumstances? What role may he play in the decisions to so invest? Similarly, under what circumstances, if any, may a board member take personal advantage of an opportunity that he learns about as a result of serving on the board?

The duty of care requires board members to act with common sense and informed judgment. It calls for a director to take an active interest in the organization's activities and not just sit back and passively "rubber stamp" decisions made by the executive staff or smaller committees of the board. Taking an active interest requires that board members attend regularly scheduled board meetings, review materials and information given to them, and evaluate appropriate courses of action. With respect to managing conflicts of interest, the duty of care requires board members to disclose their important outside interests, as discussed in detail below, and to create and enforce a mechanism by which other board members and officers must do the same. In other words, fulfilling one's duty of care includes making sure that procedures are in place so that board decisions are made in a disinterested manner, that any personal financial interests of board members are disclosed, and that individuals with personal financial interests cannot vote in favor of those interests.

Board members also must be faithful to the mission of the organization they serve — otherwise known as the duty of obedience. The duty of obedience ensures that an organization's resources and activities are being used to further its mission and not diverted to benefit private parties or to charitable purposes other than its own. The principal rationale for this responsibility is the reliance of donors on an organization's faithfulness to its purposes. These organizational principles are typically expressed in the nonprofit's certificate of incorporation, bylaws, and other documents defining the mission, including its application for recognition of tax exemption.

To ensure that they are acting in the best interest of the organization in all situations, board members need to develop a broader understanding of the different types of conflicts of interest and how they relate to the legal responsibilities of board members.

SITUATIONS THAT GIVE RISE TO CONFLICTS OF INTEREST

Most individuals are motivated by their own convictions and concerns, which naturally guide their everyday decision making. These individual interests, based in hopes and desires for themselves and others, become problematic when they, rather than the best interest of the organization, motivate board members' decisions. As discussed above, many conflicts are created by situations in which board members' personal interests collide with the organization's best interests, whether it is intentional or due to a lack of understanding of their rights and obligations.

As you will see, there are too many situations that give rise to conflicts of interest to create rigid rules. What we will do, however, is provide examples that will help guide board members when different types of conflicts are disclosed or otherwise become evident.

FINANCIAL CONFLICT

One way in which service on nonprofit boards differs markedly from the business world is that board members on for-profit boards are generally paid substantial fees. Although some private foundations do pay modest fees to board members for their board service, with rare exceptions, public charities do not offer compensation. It is understood that nonprofit board members will donate their time and resources on a purely voluntary basis to support and advance the organization's mission.

In addition to his or her board service, a board member may seek to further assist the nonprofit he or she serves further by providing goods or services to the organization at a rate well below market. As long as this relationship is disclosed to the board and the organization follows appropriate conflict-of-interest policies, it may be acceptable. (Private foundations are treated differently from public charities in this regard, as discussed in Chapter 3.) The same board member, however, may wish to use his or her position on the board to steer business to clients or relatives at above-market fees. The latter may result in a personal benefit to the board member and give rise to an impermissible conflict of interest. In the absence of a monetary reward for nonprofit board service, some board members feel they are entitled to use their position to obtain a financial benefit from the organization by, for example, entering into an advantageous transaction with the organization — individually or through a business owned by the board member, a close friend, or family member.

For example, a board member who is an architect may seek to have his architectural firm provide architectural services to an organization on whose board he serves. Whether this is acceptable will depend on the terms of any such arrangement and the due diligence process by which a firm is chosen.

A difficult situation for a board may arise where, for example, both board member Nick and board member Sally would like to do business with the organization. Nick knows that he cannot try to influence the board to enter into a transaction with his company. So he talks to Sally and they agree that Nick will promote Sally's transaction to the board, and Sally will in turn promote Nick's proposal. Where Sally and Nick are in the same line of business, and other board members are unfamiliar with that area, they may argue that they are each in the best position to evaluate the other's proposal. However, in such a situation, both Nick and Sally have an interest in both transactions and, therefore, neither one of them should participate in or seek to influence the deliberation or vote on either matter.

If a pharmacist serves on the board of a hospital, she will naturally hope that the hospital recommends to its patients that they fill their prescriptions at her pharmacy. However, an impermissible conflict arises if the hospital gives her exclusive access to its patients or recommends her pharmacy over all others. Even if the hospital does not give her exclusive access to its patients but simply promotes her pharmaceutical services, a perception of conflict may arise. When making decisions, the board must consider how such decisions will be *perceived*. Despite the absence of a legal conflict, the appearance of a conflict of interest may cause negative publicity for an organization.

A board member may seek to use his position on the board to benefit a family member. For example, if the organization that he serves grants annual awards to volunteers, the board member may recommend his daughter who is a distinguished volunteer in the community as an award recipient. If the award is a financial one, granting his daughter the award will almost certainly be unacceptable. If the award is one of recognition alone, it may be acceptable if the board member recuses himself from the decision-making process. It will depend in part on whether and to what extent such recognition is sought after and what if any other advantages come with receiving the award. If there is no limit on the number of people who can be recognized, it may be helpful to grant an award to the board member's daughter to show the extent to which the board members and their families engage in and promote volunteerism.

When a nonprofit organization continually promotes the financial interest of a board member, it may raise questions as to the individual's duty of loyalty and the extent to which the organization is impermissibly promoting a private interest. This type of situation often occurs when a nonprofit actively promotes the book and/or speaking engagements of a board member.

An extreme case in this regard involved the Central Asia Institute (CAI) and its co-founder, longtime executive director and board member, Greg Mortenson. CAI was formed to improve educational opportunities in remote regions of Pakistan and Afghanistan. Mortenson was named a finalist for the 2009 Nobel Peace Prize, and, by all accounts, his tireless devotion to CAI and its mission was substantially responsible for CAI's significant success.

Nevertheless, internal problems in the management of CAI surfaced and the Montana Attorney General conducted an investigation. One focus of the investigation involved the arrangements between CAI and Mortenson with respect to Mortenson's book *Three Cups of Tea*. The paperback version of the book was published in January 2007. It sold approximately four million copies and spent 57 weeks on the *New York Times* bestseller list.

The Montana Attorney General issued a report of its investigation of CAI and Mortenson in April 2012.[9] The report stated that CAI paid virtually all the costs of producing the book and bought and gave away thousands of copies of the book to libraries, schools, places of worship, and military installations.[10] CAI spent approximately $3.96 million in buying copies of the book[11] and also paid the advertising and travel costs for many speaking tours by Mortenson.[12] Despite CAI having paid the costs to produce *Three Cups of Tea,* CAI's board members did not know and had an inaccurate understanding of the financial details regarding the book.[13] Although Mortenson had agreed to provide a contribution to CAI to compensate it for the amount of the royalty income that Mortenson received specifically related to purchases of the book by CAI, as of early April 2011, Mortenson had not made any payments to CAI to compensate it for these royalties and the board had not taken steps to demand such payment.[14]

---

[9] Montana Attorney General, *Montana Attorney General's Investigative Report of Greg Mortenson and Central Asia Institute* (Apr. 5, 2012), available at https://files.doj.mt.gov/wp-content/uploads/2012_0405_FINAL-REPORT-FOR-DISTRIBUTION.pdf.

[10] *Id.* at 4.

[11] *Id.* at 8.

[12] *Id.* at 4.

[13] Montana Attorney General, *Montana Attorney General's Investigative Report of Greg Mortenson and Central Asia Institute, supra* note 9, at 8.

[14] *Id.* at 9.

The Montana Attorney General found that Mortenson breached his duty of loyalty to CAI because he failed to disclose to board members material facts regarding his financial interest in the books he authored, his speaking engagements, and travel reimbursements from other parties.[15] Mortenson also failed to recuse himself from votes of the board regarding significant matters that involved conflicts of interest.[16]

The Montana Attorney General entered into a settlement agreement with CAI and Mortenson.[17] Under the settlement agreement, Mortenson is required to pay CAI royalties for any books of Mortenson purchased by CAI, and he must also provide copies of any relevant contracts to CAI so CAI may determine the proper royalty amount and Mortenson must make a contribution to CAI for past royalties.[18]

One of the reasons that the CAI situation occurred was because Mortensen was such a dynamic and compelling figure that board members developed nearly blind allegiance to him. The Attorney General's report concluded that "there was a deliberate effort to put people who are loyal to Mortenson on the board. The three board members who resigned in 2002 were effectively ousted, based on tensions and conflict that had developed with Mortenson."[19] Those who resigned were trying to perform the kinds of oversight functions expected of boards of directors, such as repeatedly asking for documentation to prove that CAI was getting a positive return on the money Mortenson was spending.[20]

Some board members, particularly founders of organizations or those with a long history with the nonprofit, incorrectly have a sense of "ownership" of the organization. A key distinction between nonprofit organizations and for-profit businesses is that nonprofits have no owners — no shareholders who have a stake in the earnings of the corporation. Nevertheless, conflicts may arise because these individuals may wrongly believe that they have a right to treat the assets of the organization as their own property.

Serving as a board member while providing professional services to the organization for a fee, even a below-market fee, raises concerns for the board member filling dual roles, for the organization, and for fellow board members. Even where the board member seeks to act only in the best interests of the organization, it may be difficult

---

[15] *Id.* at 22.

[16] *Id.*

[17] *Settlement Agreement and Assurance of Voluntary Compliance, attached to Montana Attorney General, Montana Attorney General's Investigative Report of Greg Mortenson and Central Asia Institute, supra* note 9, at 1.

[18] *Id.* at 4.

[19] Montana Attorney General, *Montana Attorney General's Investigative Report of Greg Mortenson and Central Asia Institute, supra* note 9, at 17.

[20] *Id.* at 17, 18.

to give disinterested advice. In addition, if the board finds that the professional services provided are not satisfactory, raising that concern with a fellow board member may be more difficult than it would be with a service provider who is not on the board.

An investment advisor serving on a nonprofit's investment committee may encourage the organization to invest in one of his funds. He may consider it to be a great opportunity for the organization, but the nonprofit organization always must closely examine whose interests are really being served[21] and whether the investment advisor would benefit from an investment by the organization. For example, even if a board member who is an investment advisor agrees to forgo his fees, he still may be generating business for his firm, resulting in fees to his firm and whatever benefits accrue to him for generating business. The nonprofit also should make sure that it conducts the same level of due diligence with respect to funds managed by its board members as it would for funds with which the organization has no such connection.

If the advice provided by the investment manager results in inadequate investment performance for the organization — which can be easily measured — that can easily be blamed on external circumstances; fellow board members may be more receptive to explanations blaming external forces when they come from a colleague. This is particularly true if one or more of the board members also have their personal funds invested with the same investment manager. If that is the case, then the investment manager board member must be concerned with his investment performance for individual board members as well as for the organization and no longer can be focused solely on the best interests of the organization. When disagreements arise among board members, the investment manager's views may reflect the interests of the individual board members who are his clients rather than the substance of the issue involved.

With respect to legal services, it is difficult for an individual to provide first-rate, disinterested legal advice to an organization while also serving as a board member of that organization, even if the individual provides a discounted fee for her legal services. A board member must be loyal to the mission of the organization. A lawyer, on the other hand, has a broad-ranging obligation to advise, must be able to evaluate situations critically, and should not be subject to the will of the board chair or chief executive, particularly if the lawyer views the wishes of these individuals to be adverse to the interests of the organization. The role of board member and lawyer are so different that it is difficult to manage the two simultaneously.

---

[21] The New York Prudent Management of Institutional Funds Act requires a nonprofit organization's board, when delegating investment management authority to an investment manager or other external agent, to consider, among other things, the external agent's independence, including any conflicts of interest that the external agent may have.

In addition, a lawyer is not devoid of self-interest and naturally will view the organization as a whole, considering ways in which she can be of additional service. As a board member, on the other hand, the same individual may be more concerned with saving the organization's resources for its programs while viewing "legal" projects as secondary. This is a potential source of conflict.

Another conflict may occur if the lawyer does not perform well for the organization. Fellow board members may be reluctant to criticize her performance or recommend that she be replaced as the organization's counsel.

Although it once was common for nonprofit boards to rely on legal advice provided by board members and their firms, there has been a growing realization in recent years of the inherent conflicts in this process, which has resulted in a move away from this practice.

The existence of conflicting interests may fuel even unrelated board disputes. When a contentious issue arises and the board is divided, board members may seek to discredit the views of fellow directors seen as having conflicting interests, suggesting motivations other than the best interests of the organization. For example, if a disagreement occurs over a change in the organization's mission, a board member opposed to the change may be accused of favoring the status quo because it will enable him to maintain connections with certain vendors to the organization with which he has other business relationships. Such suspicions may arise whether or not the vendors are charging below-market fees and/or providing superior service to the nonprofit.

Loyalty to More Than One Nonprofit Organization

Typically, conflicts have been considered as situations where a board member has a financial interest. But, in practice, conflicting interests need not be purely financial.

As discussed above, multiple loyalties arise when a person serves on the boards of two or more nonprofit organizations at the same time. In the event that these nonprofits are considering a major transaction with each other, such as a significant grant, a joint venture, or even a merger, conflict may arise. It is extremely difficult for a board member in this case to serve both organizations with equal devotion, particularly if the board member, for whatever reason, feels a greater allegiance to the organization that will benefit most from the arrangement.

Conflicts also may result when a board member serves two different nonprofit organizations that have similar missions, serve similar constituencies, and compete for the same funding sources. If a board member has a long involvement with one of the organizations, for example, she may be known by donors as affiliated with that particular nonprofit. It may be far easier, therefore, for her to secure funding for that organization. Likewise, if she starts to fundraise for a competing entity, funders may wonder if a problem exists at the first organization, which may have caused a change in allegiance. If she seeks funds for both organizations, funders may lose faith in her recommendations. Fundraising successfully for both organizations in that circumstance can be very tricky.

This situation brings other potential conflicts as well. For example, if an individual serves on the boards of two local private schools whose students are in the same age group, the two schools may compete for students and for funding. The board member may obtain confidential information about one school that could benefit the competing school. If the board member provides this information to the competing school, he will breach his duty of loyalty to the first organization. If he does not disclose this information, however, he may be forced to participate in decisions where he has knowledge that cannot be shared with fellow board members.

A foundation board member who serves on the board of an organization that seeks funds from the foundation naturally has dual loyalties. Where a foundation board member is an employee of an organization seeking a grant, the individual's competing interests may be more difficult to sort out. Please see Chapter 4 for suggestions on how to handle these types of conflicts.

This issue of competing loyalties can arise even in the context of a supporting organization, which is organized and operated for the benefit of another tax-exempt organization. There likely will be one or more overlapping board members between the supporting organization and the organization it supports. Depending on the type of supporting organization, this may be legally required. Although the supporting organization is obligated to use its funds in furtherance of its supported organization's purposes, the supporting organization must decide how and when to do that, and may need to choose between competing demands; the individual who serves on the boards of both organizations may have difficulty determining where his duty lies in such case. Although he is obligated to vote in the best interest of the supporting organization if that is the organization whose board is voting, that may seem counterintuitive, particularly if the supported organization is the larger entity and the one running programs.

The question of loyalty to more than one organization is particularly difficult in a situation where, for example, an individual serves on the board of a cultural center *ex officio* by virtue of his or her position as president of a community development organization. Does this board member "represent" the community development organization such that she has an obligation to consider the interests of the community development organization when voting on the cultural center board? As in many of these situations, the details of the particular arrangement and the nature of the vote may affect the answer and in many cases the interests of both organizations will be aligned. In general, however, when such an individual is voting as a board member of the cultural center, she should vote in the manner she believes to be in the best interests of the cultural center. That being said, she may and likely is required to express to her fellow board members what she believes to be the interest of the community development organization and explain how, if at all, such interest diverges from the interest of the cultural center. If she feels that her dual roles make it impossible for her to be objective and clearly sort out the various interests, she should recuse herself from the vote.

CORPORATE OPPORTUNITY

It is a conflict of interest for a board member or officer to take personal advantage of a business opportunity that is offered to the organization unless the board first determines not to pursue the opportunity. If a board member obtained inside information from serving the organization, and he uses this information to, for example, outbid the organization for a property in which it has an interest, then he has violated his duty of loyalty to the organization he serves.

A board member also has a duty to disclose to the organization an opportunity in which he knows the organization would have an interest, even if it is not to his personal advantage. For example, if a museum board member who has a collection of artifacts finds out about an auction of rare objects that would be great additions to the museum's collection, he should inform representatives of the museum about the auction so that the museum has the opportunity to purchase items for its collection (even if he would be interested in the auction to add to his own collection).

In the law, this is known as the corporate opportunity doctrine, and a board member so acting to his personal advantage is seen as "appropriating a corporate opportunity." Although usually seen in the context of business corporations, courts have applied this doctrine to nonprofits and have acted to prohibit such actions and hold the board members involved responsible.

CONFLICTING ROLES AND RELATIONSHIPS

Close social relationships among board members and between board and staff can impair independence leading to conflicting interests. Where spouses, siblings, or other closely aligned people serve together on a board, questions of allegiance often arise and may create loyalties that could be given priority over a board member's legal obligations. Even more troublesome is the existence of such a close relationship between a board member and a key management employee whose performance is overseen and evaluated by the board. For family foundations, these issues are often inherent in the board structure; family foundations, for example, may not have any outside board members. Accordingly, there may be no board member who is independent of a family member whose compensation for serving as the foundation's chief executive is under consideration. Thus, these relationships may require thoughtful attention, but they can be managed effectively.

Conflicts of interest may also occur in organizations where the relationship between the board and the chief executive is poorly managed. The board and the chief executive act as both a support mechanism and check-and-balance system for the organization. The board can and should be a chief executive's most useful resource, but executives who view the board as intrusive may keep important information from the board. The risk of harmful conflicts is greater still if board members fear alienating a much needed and relied on chief executive and the board fails to look closely at the choices made by the executive, simply rubber stamping management decisions that may be of personal benefit to the executive. As a result, these board members may breach their duty of care to the organization.

Because of the nature of the relationship between the chief executive and the board, it is not advisable for a close personal friend of the chief executive to be recruited to serve on the board. It can impair the monitoring function of the board over the chief executive. For the close personal friend, the need to be objective about chief executive performance will be difficult if not impossible. If the board becomes dissatisfied with the performance of the chief executive, board members may feel inhibited in talking honestly about it in front of the chief executive's personal friend. Similarly, the board may feel constrained from confronting the chief executive about problematic conduct or taking disciplinary action against him.

In some nonprofit organizations the chief executive himself sits as a voting member of the board. Many organizations believe that denying the chief executive a seat on the board diminishes her authority and weakens management in a way that is harmful to the organization. Other organizations believe that it is not a good practice to have the chief executive serve on the board. They believe it blurs the distinction between the role of the board and that of the chief executive; instead, those organizations have their chief executives serve as ex officio nonvoting members of the board.

Attendance at board meetings in a nonvoting capacity allows the chief executive to share his perspective and professional judgment on a wide variety of issues affecting the health and future of the organization. If the chief executive serves as a voting member of the board, the board should exclude the chief executive from a discussion on the chief executive's performance or compensation.

It is generally not desirable to have the chief executive serve on a committee that has an oversight function with respect to management or with respect to the board itself. Similarly, the chief executive should not serve as board chair because he would be overseeing himself and the organization would lose the benefit of having an independent board leader.

A study of over 5,100 nonprofits conducted by the Urban Institute Center on Nonprofits and Philanthropy in years 2005–2007, included the finding that having the CEO/executive director serve as a voting member of the board results in a less engaged board and may undermine the very stewardship roles with which the board members are charged.[22]

Regardless of whether the chief executive is a voting member of the board, however, she is subject to the duties of care, loyalty, and obedience with respect to participation in board discussions.

THE CONFLICT-OF-INTEREST CONTINUUM

The examples given above demonstrate the difficulty in determining whether a given conflict of interest is a problem or not. Every human being has personal motivations and multiple loyalties. Nonprofit board members are often invited to serve precisely because of the personal and professional knowledge, experience, and connections that they bring with them. In addition to being able to recognize potential conflicts of interest, board members must be able to determine when they present areas of concern and what to do about them.

One helpful way to think about conflicts of interest is considering their place on a continuum. At one end of the continuum are conflicts that are totally unacceptable (that is, illegal or widely regarded as unethical), and at the other end are conflicts that are inconsequential. In that regard, it is important to reiterate here that not all conflicting interests are problematic. In fact, for certain organizations, their best opportunity for receiving high-quality services is through board members or those who have business or personal relationships with board members. In many instances, companies that employ board members or that are owned by board members or clients, relatives, or friends of board members may provide superior services to the organization at a fair price. Such services may include printing, construction, public relations, and Web site creation. Such conflict-of-interest transactions may be not only acceptable but also beneficial to the nonprofit organization.

The majority of conflicts of interest fall somewhere between these two extremes. The following example introduces a factual situation involving a conflicting interest, illustrating the issues a board faces when a potential conflict of interest arises, and how one conflict situation can fall in different places on the continuum depending on how it is treated and managed by the organization. It will be helpful to keep this example in mind when reviewing the legal issues in Chapter 3 and discussing the development and use of a conflict-of-interest policy in Chapter 4. Additional examples appear later in the text and in the Q&As at the end of the book.

[22] Urban Institute, Nonprofit Governance in the United States: Findings on Performance and Accountability from the First National Representative Study, 22 (2007), available at http://www.urban.org/UploadedPDF/411479_Nonprofit_Governance.pdf.

CASE STUDIES

David's Situation

David is a property developer with extensive holdings in the city. David also serves on the board of a nonprofit organization that operates into after-school programs for impoverished children. The nonprofit has just received a substantial grant that will enable it to move into a larger and more modern facility.

The board of directors of the nonprofit would like the organization to benefit from David's expertise without creating an impermissible conflict of interest. The board considers whether David may participate in strategy sessions in which the organization will determine the organization's needs and desires for the new space. The board believes this to be acceptable because no transaction yet has been proposed. However, board members must be aware of David's potential interest in obtaining the job for his company.

The board then considers whether David could serve on a committee that would solicit and review bids from multiple contractors even though David's firm would be one of the bidders. The board discusses whether it would be acceptable if David were to recuse himself from the discussion of his own firm and from voting on the final selection. However, the board recognizes two problems with this approach: First, since the purpose of the committee's work would be to compare different contractors, David would have to recuse himself from significant portions of the discussion so as not to get inside information or learn of bids by competitors; second, David may not be able to assess his competitors fairly.

To avoid having the conflict fall on the unacceptable end of the continuum, David could remain on the board but not serve on the committee and recuse himself from the full-board discussion and vote on a choice of contractor. It is not necessary for David to step down from the board.

If the bid from David's firm is the lowest bid received and David is not involved in the selection process, the conflict could fall on the acceptable side of the continuum. However, it will also be important for the board to know something about the quality of the work provided by David's firm. If David's firm has done work for the organization previously, that would, of course, be the best way for the organization to judge the firm's performance. It is also possible that one or more board members may have had direct personal experience with David's work. Although board members may know David well and may trust him, the board is still required to conduct the due diligence about his firm that would be required of any potential contractor.

Michael's Situation

Similar concerns arise when board member Michael serves on a task force that is charged with preparing a job description for the organization's next chief executive, identifying the needs of the organization in its next phase of operations. As he participates in this process, Michael decides that this is a great opportunity, one which he himself wishes to pursue. When Michael applies for the job, other task force members wonder whether Michael argued for elements of the job description that matched his own experience. Would the task force report look the same if Michael had not become interested in the chief executive position? Board members who review potential candidates and interview finalists will need to keep this in mind during the process, and Michael should not participate.

As these examples illustrate, board members must be prepared to recognize potential conflicts of interest, raise questions about them, discuss them openly, and take action to prevent them from becoming unacceptable conflicts. Board members must recognize that their overall goal is not to avoid conflicts of interest completely — that is impossible. Helping their organizations in managing these conflicts appropriately when they arise begins with the creation of clear procedures for unearthing the relevant outside interests of board members. This requires that all officers and directors be subject to a disclosure requirement and that the organization has a clear conflict-of-interest policy, setting forth exactly what interests must be made known. The policy must describe the mechanism for reporting conflicts, and identify the person or group to whom conflicts should be reported. Finally, the policy must describe how determinations are made as to where on the continuum the conflict of interest falls.

If the individual board member will obtain a personal benefit from a proposed transaction with the organization that he or she serves and the organization could enter into a more advantageous transaction without the conflict, then the organization must look seriously at whether it may enter into such transaction. If the proposed transaction involving a board member is equally advantageous to the organization as other available arrangements, there may be reasons to choose the transaction involving the board member. The organization may have confidence in the competence of the board member or her company based on past experience or personal recommendations and may know the board member to be an honest and reliable person. Such specific knowledge should be factored into any decision as to what will be best for the organization.

It is useful to set out some of the other legal concepts that must be understood in connection with making these determinations. Because there are so many ways in which conflicts arise and because they can cause great harm to an organization if not addressed, it is critical that board members and executive staff have a general understanding of the laws governing conflicts, and appreciate the need to implement and enforce a conflicts policy.

CHAPTER 3
Conflicts of Interest and the Law

Every board member has the responsibility for recognizing and disclosing conflicts that, if not properly addressed, could subject the organization to unfavorable public scrutiny, investigations by regulatory agencies, and/or the imposition of financial or other penalties. For this reason, board members need to develop a basic understanding of the state and federal laws that are implicated in conflict-of-interest transactions in nonprofits. Doing so will help board members recognize legally tenuous conflict-of-interest situations and ensure that the organization consults with a legal expert as needed.

STATE LAWS

Until recently, conflicts of interest were governed almost entirely by state law which, in general, is the law that applies to the conduct of directors of corporations, whether business or nonprofit. The three legal duties described in Chapter 2 are set out in state statutes and in decisions of state courts.

As discussed previously, the key concept underlying state conflict statutes and state legal decisions dealing with conflicts is the duty of loyalty. State laws do not have a comprehensive formulation of the duty of loyalty, but many states do have specific statutes that capture one or more aspects of it. In New York, for example, the compensation of officers and directors must be reasonable and commensurate with the services performed. Additionally, many states absolutely prohibit loans to officers and directors.

Most state statutes do not prohibit conflicting interest transactions, but regulate how decisions should be made regarding specific transactions. State statutes allow approval of contracts or transactions by a board or board committee where the members are disinterested and aware of the nature of any conflicting interests that exist, so that decisions are both disinterested and informed. For example, if a board member owns a company that is entering into a contract with the nonprofit organization (one that is not a private foundation), those reviewing the contract must know of the board member's ownership interest, and the interested board member's vote may not be counted in the vote to approve or disapprove the contract.

State conflict statutes also commonly stipulate that a contract or transaction between an organization and a board member or officer cannot be challenged if it is fair to the organization, regardless of the circumstances surrounding its approval. The fairness of transactions is usually analyzed by comparing them with similar transactions negotiated by unrelated parties dealing at arm's length — in other words, parties that have no other relationship to each other and, therefore, are presumed to make decisions based on rational economic interests. For instance, depending upon what alternatives are available, a public charity may be able to retain the services of a real estate agent who is a board member or the spouse of a board member if the services are provided at or below the market rate.

Some state laws, including California and a number of states that have adopted a model state corporation law, impose a requirement that before approving any transaction involving a conflicting interest, the board must satisfy itself that the organization could not obtain a more advantageous arrangement with reasonable effort from parties without a conflict. Thus, for example, an organization could not lease a copier from an office equipment rental company owned by a board member if it could enter into a lease on more favorable terms with another office equipment rental company owned by someone who was not a member of the board. State statutes generally apply to all nonprofit organizations incorporated in the state, although specific provisions may apply only to "charitable" or other specific types of nonprofit organizations.

FEDERAL TAX LAW

Federal tax law contains two complementary doctrines that fundamentally differentiate nonprofit organizations from their for-profit counterparts: private inurement and private benefit. Both are rooted in the concept that nonprofit organizations must be organized and operated to serve the public interest and not for personal gain.

PRIVATE INUREMENT

Tax-exempt charitable organizations have no owners. All of the organization's assets, including any net revenues, must be used for the organization's tax-exempt purposes. Federal tax law prohibits such organizations from transferring any money or other property to "insiders" as if they were owners whether through excessive compensation, by overpaying for goods or services, or in some other way. If an organization insider does receive an impermissible financial benefit from a transaction with the organization, that benefit, however small, may jeopardize the organization's tax-exempt status. This ban on inurement extends to public charities and private foundations, as well as social welfare organizations, business leagues, chambers of commerce, real estate boards, social clubs, and several other types of tax-exempt organizations. In short, these exempt organizations must serve a public interest, and therefore may not be organized or operated for the benefit of insiders.

Traditionally, an organization's officers, board members, and founders, as well as their families, have been considered insiders. Additionally, the IRS has held that any individual who has a significant influence over the organization's operations — such as a chief executive officer — may be treated as an insider for purposes of deciding whether an organization has engaged in transactions that would be viewed as involving prohibited inurement. The perceived danger is that those who have the opportunity to direct the organization's resources may divert these resources to themselves or entities that they control or in which they have an interest.

The position of the IRS is that "even a modicum of inurement can cause loss of exemption." The rules on inurement, however, do not prohibit insiders from being paid reasonable salaries for services rendered — even including bonuses in some circumstances — or from engaging in transactions on terms favorable to the tax-exempt organization.

Private foundations are also subject to self-dealing regulations, which further limit transactions between private foundations and their board members, foundation managers, and others. (See the section "Self-Dealing Rules Applicable to Private Foundations" on page 34.)

PRIVATE BENEFIT

The private benefit doctrine, applicable to all charitable organizations, is similar to the inurement doctrine but is not limited to situations where benefits are given to insiders. Private benefit is based on the rule that certain exempt organizations are created to serve broad charitable purposes and not to benefit private individuals, except to an insubstantial extent.

Private benefit may be acceptable and considered insubstantial when it is incidental to the organization's pursuit of its tax-exempt purposes. A private benefit will be considered incidental and, therefore, acceptable if it is a necessary part of the activity that benefits the public at large, as long as the benefit to the public cannot be achieved without necessarily benefiting certain individuals. For example, when an organization preserved and improved a lake for public recreational purposes with funds from adjoining landowners and others in the community, the IRS ruled that the organization was tax exempt even though the project was also benefiting private lakefront property owners. The benefit to these private owners was not the goal of the project, but it would be impossible for the organization to accomplish its purposes without also benefiting these property owners. Therefore, their benefit is incidental to the betterment of the lake for the public in improving a recreational site.[23]

---

[23] Rev. Rul. 70-186; 1970-1 CB 128.

INTERMEDIATE SANCTIONS RULES

Tax-exempt organizations that are described in Sections 501(c)(3) and 501(c)(4) of the Internal Revenue Code (the Code) — except for private foundations, which are governed by different rules (see the section "Self-Dealing Rules Applicable to Private Foundations" on page 34) — are now subject to what have become known as the intermediate sanctions rules of Code Section 4958. These intermediate sanctions rules were created to give the IRS a way to deal with abuses of the privilege of tax exemption without having to revoke the tax exemption of otherwise legitimate organizations.

Intermediate sanctions give a more concrete definition to the basic notion of private inurement, although, as described below, the definitions may differ and the intermediate sanctions rules do not address revocation of an organization's tax exemption. These rules, which were added to federal tax law in 1996, provide for a system of penalty taxes to be imposed on disqualified persons who receive a personal benefit from excess benefit transactions and on certain organization managers approving such transactions. They also provide a safe harbor for those organization managers who meet certain conditions related to decision making and documentation. (For more information, see the section "Penalties for Excess Benefit Transactions" on page 30.)

The intermediate sanctions rules address, among other things, the payment of compensation to a disqualified person and the sale or lease of property or purchase of services by an organization to or from a disqualified person. A disqualified person is an individual who is in a position to exercise substantial influence over the organization at any time during a five-year period, which ends on the date the transaction at issue occurred (such as when an employment contract was entered into or a closing took place on a sale of property). For example, a former chief executive, who resigned only two years earlier, is still treated as a disqualified person if she engages in a transaction with the organization. That explains why the Form 990 asks questions about interested-party transactions with current or former officers, directors, trustees, and key employees.

While the definition of "disqualified person" is directed specifically at members of the organization's governing board and their families (ancestors, descendants, siblings, and their respective spouses), as well as senior staff members (presidents, chief executives, chief financial officers, chief operating officers), it can extend to anyone who can exercise substantial influence over an organization. This may include a substantial contributor to the organization — someone who contributed more than $5,000, if $5,000 represents more than 2 percent of total contributions to the organization received during the organization's current taxable year and the four preceding taxable years — and anyone who manages a discrete segment or activity of an organization that represents a substantial portion of the organization's activities, assets, income, or expenses (e.g., the head of a hospital cardiology department who is a major source of patient revenue). Corporations and partnerships in which disqualified persons and their family members own more than 35 percent of the total voting power or profits interest are also treated as disqualified persons.

The definition of disqualified person is similar to that of "insider" for inurement purposes, but the definitions are not identical. The intermediate sanctions rules define the term "disqualified persons" with great specificity, detailing categories of individuals who are or are not disqualified persons and providing examples of facts and circumstances suggesting that individuals do or do not exercise the requisite substantial influence. Most disqualified persons, of course, are or were insiders (or are related to them in some way). It is possible that over time the meaning of "insider" for inurement purposes may be determined with reference to the disqualified person definitions under the intermediate sanctions rules.

EXCESS BENEFIT TRANSACTIONS

Under the intermediate sanctions rules, an excess benefit transaction occurs when the value of the economic benefit provided (directly or indirectly) by the tax-exempt organization to any disqualified person exceeds the value of the consideration (including the performance of services) received by the tax-exempt organization for providing such benefit.

Unreasonable Compensation as Excess Benefit Transaction

An excess benefit transaction occurs when an organization pays unreasonable compensation to a disqualified person. The compensation of the chief executive officer, chief financial officer, or, perhaps, that of a critical department head, is most often at issue. A determination of whether compensation is reasonable is made by comparing the amount of compensation with the amount that ordinarily would be paid by like entities (whether taxable or tax exempt) under similar circumstances (see the section "Rebuttable Presumption of Reasonableness" on page 31). Compensation for purposes of determining reasonableness includes all economic benefits (pension, insurance, etc.) provided in exchange for the performance of services. While there is an exception for an initial contract with, for example, a chief executive with no prior relationship to the organization, any material change in this sort of arrangement (such as a change in payment terms that is more than incidental, or a mutual extension of the agreement) does not satisfy the exception and, therefore, would be subject to the rules.

Non–Fair-Market-Value Purchase of Property or Services as Excess Benefit Transaction

Purchases of property and services are also subject to the intermediate sanctions rules. When an organization purchases property or professional services from a disqualified person, a member of a disqualified person's family, or a corporation in which the disqualified person owns more than 35 percent, the organization must purchase at or below fair market value in order to avoid an excess benefit transaction. In other words, if an officer or board member seeks to sell property or provide services to the nonprofit organization either individually or through a company that he or she owns, such transaction is regulated by the excess benefit transaction rules. If the organization pays more than fair market value, it has provided an excess benefit to the disqualified person from whom the property is purchased or whose services are used.

PENALTIES FOR EXCESS BENEFIT TRANSACTIONS

Intermediate sanctions, as defined in Code Section 4958, impose penalties in the form of excise taxes on the disqualified person or persons who receive the excess benefits and on organization managers (usually board members) who participate in the approval of the transaction, knowing it to be an excess benefit transaction. (Organization managers include officers, board members, and anyone having similar powers or responsibilities, regardless of title.) No penalties are incurred by the organization itself.

First and foremost, the excess benefit transaction must be corrected, or in other words, the excess benefit must be repaid to the exempt organization (see discussion below). Penalty excise taxes are still imposed even though the excess benefit has been repaid.

Tax on Disqualified Person

The initial penalty on the disqualified person who receives an excess benefit is 25 percent of the value of the excess benefit. So, for example, if a chief executive is paid a salary of $250,000 per year and reasonable pay should be only $150,000, the excess benefit is $100,000 and the penalty to be paid by the executive will be $25,000. With respect to a sale of property or provision of paid services by a disqualified person to an applicable organization, the excess benefit would be the amount by which the price exceeds the fair market value of the property or services.

In either case, if the transaction is not corrected in a timely manner, a second penalty of 200 percent of the excess may be imposed. In the example above, the second penalty would be $200,000 (twice the $100,000 excess).

"Correcting" a transaction means undoing the excess benefit to the extent possible and taking any additional measures to place the organization in a financial position no worse than it would have been had the transaction not awarded an excess benefit to the disqualified person. The correction amount is the total excess benefit amount, plus interest. In this case, the chief executive's salary would need to be reduced to a fair level — that is, to the level considered reasonable ($150,000) to avoid future excess benefit transactions.

Tax on Organization Manager

Again, an organization manager can include officers, board members, or anyone having similar authority or responsibilities. Code Section 4958 imposes a 10 percent penalty on an organization manager who knowingly participates in an excess benefit transaction by, for example, knowingly voting to approve an excess salary or failing to act or speak up when under a duty to do so. The maximum total amount of tax collectable from organization managers with respect to any one excess benefit transaction currently is $20,000. If the board has met the intermediate sanctions' safe-harbor requirements for acting on conflicting interest transactions (known as the rebuttable presumption of reasonableness), the managers would ordinarily not be subject to the tax penalty.

REBUTTABLE PRESUMPTION OF REASONABLENESS

The intermediate sanctions rules outline a safe harbor whereby nonprofit leaders can show that they have taken appropriate steps to determine that the terms of a transaction with a disqualified person are reasonable. This safe harbor is known as the rebuttable presumption of reasonableness. These procedures also provide a road map for nonprofit leaders who wish to ensure that they are acting appropriately with respect to such transactions.[24]

A compensation arrangement is presumed to be "reasonable" and a transfer of property is presumed to be at fair market value if the following conditions are met:

1. The terms of the compensation arrangement or the property transfer are approved in advance by an authorized body of the organization composed entirely of individuals who do not have a conflict of interest with respect to the compensation arrangement or property transfer (in other words, they must be independent).

2. The authorized body obtained and relied upon appropriate data allowing a fair comparison to be made prior to its determination.

3. The authorized body adequately documented the basis for its decision when making it.

---

[24] Although there has been some legislative discussion of eliminating the presumption of reasonableness, it remains in place at this time. Even if any change were made, the steps outlined above that currently create the presumption almost certainly would be retained as standards of due diligence and good governance.

An authorized body may be the governing body (i.e., board of directors), a committee of the governing body (if permitted by state law), or others in some circumstances. The authorized body is not independent if any of its members is a subordinate of the person with the conflict or has other material interests in the potential outcome of the arrangement.

A joint approval arrangement, whereby an individual approves compensation of the disqualified person and the disqualified person, in turn, approves that individual's compensation or a transaction providing economic benefits to such individual, does not satisfy the independence requirement. However, if an individual who serves on the board, or on a committee that is acting as the authorized body, is conflicted in one of the ways described above, he may meet with the other members of the governing body to answer questions and then recuse himself from the meeting before a vote takes place. In a case like this, the authorized body will still meet the independence requirement.

In the case of property and professional services, appropriate data as to comparability include, for example, current independent appraisals of the property to be transferred or offers received as part of a bidding process. Relevant information on compensation includes compensation paid by similarly situated organizations, both taxable and tax exempt, for functionally comparable positions; the availability of similar services in the geographic area of the organization; current compensation surveys compiled by independent firms; and written offers from similar institutions competing for the services of the disqualified person.

If the requirements of the rebuttable presumption are satisfied, then the IRS must develop sufficient contrary evidence to rebut, or disprove, the comparability data relied upon by the board or other authorized body.

EXCESS BENEFIT TRANSACTIONS AND MAINTENANCE OF TAX EXEMPT STATUS

Generally, Code Section 501(c)(3) and the accompanying regulations establish certain tests that an organization must meet to qualify for tax-exempt status, including the prohibition against private inurement. The intermediate sanctions rules, on the other hand, do not address the tax-exempt status of organizations but, instead, impose tax penalties on disqualified persons and certain organization managers. The IRS consistently has taken the position that the imposition of excise taxes under the intermediate sanctions rules does not foreclose revocation of tax-exempt status in appropriate cases.

In May 2008, the IRS issued final regulations addressing the question of whether an organization will retain tax-exempt status if it engages in one or more excess benefit transactions that also violate the prohibition on inurement. These regulations provide that in determining whether to continue to recognize the tax-exempt status of an organization that engages in one or more excess benefit transactions (that also violate the prohibition on inurement), the IRS will consider all relevant facts and circumstances, including, but not limited to

1. the size and scope of the organization's regular and ongoing activities that further exempt purposes before and after the excess benefit transaction(s) occurred

2. the size and scope of the excess benefit transaction or transactions (collectively, if more than one) in relation to the size and scope of the organization's regular and ongoing activities that further exempt purposes

3. whether the organization has been involved in multiple excess benefit transactions

4. whether the organization has implemented safeguards that are reasonably calculated to prevent future violations

5. whether the excess benefit transaction has been corrected or the organization has made good-faith efforts to seek correction from the disqualified persons who benefited from the excess benefit transaction

With respect to number four above — the implementation of safeguards that are reasonably calculated to prevent future violations — a key safeguard cited in nearly every example is the adoption of a conflict-of-interest policy. The regulations provide that the factors in numbers four and five above will weigh more heavily in favor of continuing to recognize exemption where the organization discovers the excess benefit transaction and takes action before the IRS discovers the excess benefit transaction. Here again is evidence of how important it is for an organization to develop policies and procedures to uncover problematic interested party transactions and either prevent them from occurring or take corrective actions if they do.

EXCESS BENEFIT TRANSACTION RULES APPLICABLE TO SUPPORTING ORGANIZATIONS AND DONOR ADVISED FUNDS

The Pension Protection Act of 2006 extended the excess benefit transaction rules to excess benefit transactions between a donor advised fund and its disqualified persons and also between an organization sponsoring donor advised funds and its disqualified persons.[25] When designing a conflict-of-interest policy, a donor advised fund should consider the special rules applicable to it.

---

[25] Generally, a donor advised fund is a separately identified fund or account that is maintained and operated by a section 501(c)(3) organization, which is called a sponsoring organization. Each account is composed of contributions made by individual donors. Once the donor makes the contribution, the organization has legal control over it. However, the donor, or the donor's representative, retains advisory privileges with respect to the distribution of funds and the investment of assets in the account.

Similarly, the Pension Protection Act contains specific provisions applicable to organizations classified as supporting organizations under Section 509(a)(3) of the Code. Supporting organizations are charities that carry out their exempt purposes by supporting other exempt organizations, usually other public charities. Supporting organizations are treated differently from other public charities in part because they may be funded by a small number of persons in a manner similar to a private foundation. Under the Pension Protection Act, any grant, loan, compensation, or other similar payment from a supporting organization to a substantial contributor of the supporting organization, a related person of the substantial contributor, or a 35 percent controlled entity of a substantial contributor or any of the substantial contributor's family members is treated as an automatic excess benefit transaction, subject to excise tax penalties. In addition, any loan from a supporting organization to a disqualified person of the supporting organization is treated as an automatic excess benefit transaction, subject to excise tax penalties. Accordingly, supporting organizations should review the details of these rules so that their conflict policies are designed to require disclosure of any proposed transactions prohibited under these rules.

SELF-DEALING RULES APPLICABLE TO PRIVATE FOUNDATIONS

The intermediate sanctions rules do not apply to private foundations; instead, private foundations are subject to an even stricter set of self-dealing rules that became law as part of the Tax Reform Act of 1969. The Act created the distinction between private foundations and public charities.

The Code (and accompanying regulations) prohibit as self-dealing many transactions between a foundation and a disqualified person. The definition of disqualified person under the private foundation rules is similar but not identical to that under the intermediate sanctions rules. Disqualified persons for self-dealing purposes include members of the board, officers, and their family members (but only spouses, ancestors, children, grandchildren, great-grandchildren, and their spouses; not siblings, nieces and nephews, aunts and uncles, cousins, or other more distant relatives). Disqualified persons also include any corporation, partnership, trust, or estate in which any of these people has more than 35 percent of the voting power, profits interest, or beneficial interest.

Under the self-dealing rules, there is no fair-market-value test. If a transaction is prohibited self-dealing, it makes no difference whether the terms of the deal are at fair market value or are otherwise beneficial to the private foundation. The following transactions between a private foundation and a disqualified person constitute prohibited self-dealing:

- the sale or exchange, or leasing, of property between a private foundation and a disqualified person

- lending of money or other extension of credit between a private foundation and a disqualified person (except loans by the disqualified person to the foundation without interest when all proceeds are used for charitable purposes)

- furnishing of goods, services, or facilities between a private foundation and a disqualified person (except that a disqualified person may furnish goods, services, or facilities to a foundation without charge as long as the goods, services, or facilities are used for charitable purposes)

- payment of compensation or payment or reimbursement of expenses by a private foundation to a disqualified person (except that reasonable compensation may be paid for personal services rendered by disqualified persons)

- transfer to, use by, or for the benefit of a disqualified person of the income or assets of the foundation

As indicated above, the self-dealing rules do allow reimbursement for reasonable expenses and payment of reasonable compensation to board members, officers, and employees for services performed to promote or fulfill the mission of the organization. It is also permissible to make payments for certain professional services such as legal and investment counseling services. However, arrangements such as using a board member's firm as a vendor for the foundation's copying machines or leasing office space from a board member is strictly forbidden. That said, board members may provide goods and services (e.g., office space, equipment, or administrative staff) free of charge to the foundation.

As with the excess benefit transaction rules for public charities (which were modeled on the self-dealing rules for private foundations), the Code imposes a two-tier system of taxes on both the disqualified person who engages in an act of self-dealing and on any foundation manager who knowingly participates in the transaction. No self-dealing tax is imposed on the foundation itself. The initial tax on the disqualified person is equal to 10 percent of the amount involved in the transaction and any foundation manager who knowingly participated in the act is taxed at 5 percent of the amount involved (subject to a $20,000 limit). If the violation is not corrected in a timely manner, the taxes increase to 200 percent and 50 percent, respectively, with a maximum additional tax on any foundation manager of $10,000 for any one act.

Even if an activity does not violate the prohibition against self-dealing, it may be a conflict of interest that carries other risks to the foundation and its board members and managers. Thus, it should be managed properly in accordance with the organization's conflict-of-interest policy.

OTHER LAWS

Many organizations receive funding from federal agencies. Awards like these are covered by rules of the federal Office of Management and Budget (OMB). OMB rules allow a federal funding agency to recoup grant funds if they are expended by an organization in ways that violate OMB rules. OMB rules prohibit an employee or officer from participating in the award or administration of a contract supported by federal funds if a real or apparent conflict interest would be involved. Such a conflict would arise when the employee or officer, any member of his or her immediate family, or his or her partner, has a financial or other interest in the firm selected for an award. Many local governments also have rules against awarding contracts to organizations whose board members have conflicting interests.

Understanding the requirements and restrictions imposed by state laws and the intermediate sanctions rules, and ensuring that the organization complies with them, is a significant part of the duty of care that board members owe to an organization. The complexity of federal and state law, however, means that consultation with a legal professional is also an essential part of board members' duty of care.

CHAPTER 4

The Conflict-of-Interest Policy: Addressing Conflicts before Problems Arise

The most effective way to prevent conflicts of interest from becoming problematic is to take a proactive approach to managing them. Such an approach involves creating an environment that promotes open communication, transparency, and accountability among board members and staff. The board chair should encourage all board members to be open about any concerns they may have, especially if those concerns involve potential conflicts of interest among board members or staff. Developing a diverse board is also useful to ensure a variety of viewpoints and enhance independence among board members. The success of these other efforts depends, however, on the establishment and enforcement of a conflict-of-interest policy and a disclosure procedure.

The organization also may wish to create a policy for the promotion of ethical conduct to encourage volunteers and staff to act with honesty and integrity and to treat each other with respect (please see Chapter 6 for more information). This document should be separate from the conflict-of-interest policy, but both should be distributed to board members and officers together as part of the organization's package of key documents.

DIVERSITY ON THE BOARD: AN ESSENTIAL COMPONENT

When relatives, friends, and/or business partners serve together on a nonprofit board, it is generally more likely that conflicts of interest will arise and be more difficult to resolve. A small board made up of family members and friends might not be able to recognize conflict-of-interest problems. Additionally, if a board member does spot a potential problem, he or she might feel that bringing it to the attention of others would not be productive or would damage personal ties.

It is helpful, therefore, in preventing conflicts to have board members who come from different backgrounds and have varying points of view. This may not be appropriate, of course, for small family foundations. Family members are generally the most familiar with the intent of the original donor even after he or she has died or is no longer involved. In the case of public charities and larger private foundations, however, the board chair should promote recruitment of new board members with diverse perspectives.

CREATING THE POLICY

It is important for board members to be generally familiar with the laws discussed in the previous chapter. It is unrealistic, however, to expect every board member to understand all of the intricacies of these laws, how precisely they apply in every given situation, and how state and federal laws may overlap and/or differ in their application. Therefore, it is critical for organizations to develop a conflict-of-interest policy that is understandable and that includes a disclosure requirement for board members. A good conflict-of-interest policy is meant as a guide to aid nonprofit directors and officers in fulfilling their duty of loyalty. It should promote transparency and openness in the organization. The conflict policy does not replace or serve as a substitute for state or federal law but it facilitates the exercise of good governance practices and helps board members avoid violations of the legal prohibitions, with the help of legal counsel, when appropriate.

Boards may handle the creation of a conflict-of-interest policy in a variety of ways. A special committee of the board may be established to prepare and monitor compliance with the policy. Alternatively, if there is a governance committee or if governance is a function of the nominating committee, then that committee in charge of governance issues may be responsible for creating and monitoring the conflict-of-interest policy. An independent audit committee can also serve effectively in monitoring and enforcing the conflicts policy. In developing the policy, the committee may wish to seek input from other board members, but the committee should remain in control of the drafting process. In addition, executive staff members are often involved in the process of developing and implementing conflict-of-interest policies, but the burden of approval and compliance rests with the board.

Because of the importance of legal issues in formulating a policy, the organization's legal counsel must also be involved in creating the policy itself and/or reviewing a draft created by the committee. The conflict-of-interest policy should then be presented to the board for review and approval. Board members should have time to review the details of the policy and to ask questions regarding its terms and whether or not it covers certain situations.

Once the policy is adopted, it must be treated as a living document and used — not put on a shelf and forgotten. The board chair, or another designated board member, should bring a copy of the conflict policy to every board meeting, and the policy should be referred to as necessary in the same way as are the organization's bylaws. Additionally, review and discussion of the conflict-of-interest policy and completion of a disclosure statement should be part of every new board member's orientation. Both the IRS and the state's attorney general look not only at whether an organization has a conflict-of-interest policy but also how well an organization adheres to that policy.

Because the conflict-of-interest policy is such an important governance tool, each nonprofit board should develop one that serves its particular environment and circumstances. Appendix 2 contains the sample conflict-of-interest policy that the IRS provides as an acceptable policy for new organizations seeking recognition of tax-exempt status: Although this policy lists the information that should be included in an annual statement by each director, principal officer, and member of a committee with governing board delegated powers, the policy does not include a form of annual disclosure statement so any organization using the IRS policy must create its own annual disclosure statement. Appendix 3 provides a more detailed sample policy. Adopting a simpler policy like the IRS sample is a useful way for a new organization, a smaller organization, or one without an established board or board committees, to introduce the issue of conflicting interests and the need for disclosure. More mature organizations should consider developing a more detailed policy like the sample provided in Appendix 3. This sample policy accomplishes the intended goals well, but should be used as merely a starting document for boards to use to facilitate development of their own specific policies.

As described above, when designing a conflict policy, donor advised funds and supporting organizations should consider the special excess benefit transaction rules applicable to each of those types of organizations respectively.

A conflict-of-interest policy for a private foundation must address the specific concerns of foundations, including the IRS self-dealing rules and grantmaking issues. The first consideration for a private foundation is whether a proposed transaction is prohibited under the IRS self-dealing rules that are described in Chapter 3. If there is no self-dealing violation, then the transaction should be analyzed in accordance with the sample policies provided in the appendices and as reviewed in this chapter.

The true test of any conflict policy is how well it is understood and, therefore, how well it serves to surface and address actual conflicts within an organization. Experience undoubtedly will lead to the refinement of any conflict policy. If an organization has a conflict-of-interest policy but it is not surfacing the information needed to identify conflicts or, alternatively, if conflicts are disclosed but not addressed, then the policy and enforcement process must be reviewed and modified accordingly. Every conflict-of-interest policy, even those that appear to be effective, should be evaluated every three to five years to make sure that they are current.

The Urban Institute study cited above in the discussion of conflicting roles and relationships in Chapter 2, reported that 21 percent of nonprofits reported buying or renting goods, services, or property from a board member or affiliated company during the previous two years.[26] For nonprofits with annual expenses of more than $10 million, that figure rose to more than 41 percent.[27] However, among the nonprofits reporting that they did not engage in transactions with board members or affiliated companies, 75 percent also reported that they do not require board members to disclose their financial interests in entities doing business with the organization and therefore they may have been unaware of existing transactions.[28]

Among respondents of the Urban Institute study, only half reported having a written conflict-of-interest policy and only 29 percent required disclosure of financial interests.[29] Accordingly, many organizations can do more to protect themselves against conflicts of interest that result in transactions that are financially disadvantageous to the organization and provide benefits to one or more individuals who have substantial influence over the organization.

It is best to create a conflict-of-interest policy as a stand-alone document rather than try to incorporate it into the organization's bylaws. The board may, however, wish to insert a clause in the bylaws that references the requirement that board members adhere to the conflict-of-interest policy.

CASE STUDY: THE HOLYOKE MEDICAL CENTER

Following a 2008 inquiry of Holyoke Medical Center, Inc. (the Medical Center), the Public Charities Division of the Massachusetts Office of the Attorney General (the Division) emphasized the importance of evaluating conflicts of interest in accordance with an organization's established procedure.[30] The Division reviewed matters related to transactions in which the Medical Center purchased insurance coverage through the brokerage services of an insurance agency owned in part by one of the Medical Center's directors. The Medical Center purchased most (but not all) of its lines of insurance coverage through the insurance agency. The Division did not evaluate whether the transactions were or were not in the best interests of the Medical Center. The Division concluded, however, that the Medical Center failed to comply in all material respects with its long-standing written policies and procedures governing conflicts of interest. The Division concluded that the insurance transactions were covered by the Medical Center's conflict-of-interest policy and that

---

[26] Urban Institute, *Nonprofit Governance in the United States: Findings on Performance and Accountability from the First National Representative Study, supra* note 22, at 8.

[27] *Id.*

[28] *Id.*

[29] Urban Institute, *Nonprofit Governance in the United States: Findings on Performance and Accountability from the First National Representative Study, supra* note 22, at 9.

[30] Massachusetts Attorney General, *Letter to Members of the Board of Directors of Holyoke Medical Center, Inc. re: Related Party Transactions/Conflicts of Interest* (Nov. 25, 2008), available at http://www.mass.gov/ago/docs/nonprofit/holyoke-medical-112508.pdf.

the director disclosed her financial interest in the insurance company on her annual disclosure statements. However, the Division found that neither the Medical Center's board nor any committee evaluated, reviewed, or discussed the director's disclosure statements to determine whether a conflict existed, or reviewed, acted on, made findings regarding, or approved the insurance purchases.

The Medical Center agreed to the following recommendations made by the Division:

1. The board of directors, with the assistance of counsel, will review (i) the role and operations of the conflict of interest committee and (ii) the conflict of interest policy and the form of disclosure statement to assure that the conflict of interest committee has the power and procedures necessary to perform its role and to assure that the conflict of interest policy provides for a process sufficient to assure that all related party transactions are in the best interest of the Medical Center.

2. The board of directors, or the committee, will review all current disclosure statements to assure that all directors, officers, and members of senior management have made current filings and each disclosed financial interest has been evaluated by the committee consistent with the policy.

3. The Medical Center, with the assistance of an outside independent insurance consultant, will initiate a competitive bidding process for insurance brokerage services for all lines of insurance coverage in which a related party may benefit.

WHO SHOULD BE COVERED BY THE POLICY?

An organization's first step in designing a conflict-of-interest policy is to determine whom the policy will cover. Given the broad reach of the intermediate sanctions rules and the state law fiduciary obligations of directors and officers, a conflict policy must cover an organization's board members and officers. In addition, an organization should identify those employees who are in a position to exercise substantial influence over the affairs of the organization, even if they do not have a formal officer's title, and should include the job titles related to those positions (for example, executive director, chief executive officer, chief operating officer, and chief financial officer). In nonprofit organizations, many of the individuals who have such titles as president, vice president, and treasurer are volunteers who serve on the governing board, and the actual functions of those offices are carried out by staff members who typically are not officers. Those staff members should be covered by the policy as well.

As described above, under the intermediate sanctions rules, disqualified persons retain that status for a period of five years after they leave a position that gave them substantial influence over the organization. Accordingly, some organizations choose to draft their conflict policies to cover individuals for that period as well.

Because of the self-dealing rules applicable to private foundations, private foundations should identify those employees who, although technically not officers, have powers or responsibilities similar to those of officers or directors (for example, a chief executive) as well as the foundation's substantial contributors. All of those individuals are considered disqualified persons under the private foundation self-dealing rules.

If an organization wishes to create rules on conflicting interests for staff members who are not key decision makers, it is best to include them in the organization's employee handbook, rather than in a separate conflicts policy. Most employees have neither the opportunity nor the authority to make the kinds of decisions and take the kinds of actions that conflicts policies are intended to cover. Therefore, it makes the most sense for additional policies applying to staffers to be included with other rules on employee conduct.

To Whom Are Conflicting Interests Reported?

This key question for every organization has two parts: First, who should be responsible for collecting, reading, and retaining board and staff disclosure statements? Second, if a conflict arises between the filing of annual disclosure statements, how and to whom should this conflict be reported?

A good option is a committee of the board — either one that is specifically charged with dealing with conflicts, or a more general governance committee, which also may be responsible for the organization's bylaws and other governance matters. The best approach will depend on the overall size and structure of the organization, but it is a good idea for the responsible group or committee to involve the board chair in handling reported conflicts. Some boards designate a compliance officer (or conflicts officer) who both monitors disclosure statements and serves as the point person when interim conflicts arise. The compliance officer may be the chair of the group or committee charged with handling conflicts.

The compliance officer should collect disclosure statements from new board members and staff who are covered by the policy, and should ensure that statements of current board and staff members are updated annually and in between annual filings, if significant organizational changes occur that pose a possibility of a conflict. In large organizations, a lawyer in the counsel's office may handle the collection of statements from new individuals, as well as other compliance responsibilities.

If an individual has been designated to receive reports of conflicts in the first instance, he or she can then refer the issue to a governance committee, an executive committee, an audit committee, or the full board. Alternatively, there may be a board committee that has decision-making authority over the substantive matter in question. As we discuss later, many conflicts of interests are situational, and may become evident during a board meeting. Under those circumstances, the affected board member needs to disclose the conflict to the chair, who needs to take action to ensure that the appropriate process is followed to resolve the situation.

Although collecting and reviewing conflict of interest disclosure statements may seem like a ministerial function, it is the most critical aspect of the conflict management process. All of the forms must be collected and reviewed. Where a board member's company has been providing services to the organization for a long time, such as in the case of the Holyoke Medical Center described above, there may be a tendency not to bring the matter to the relevant committee or full board. However, the sheer length of time such services have been provided without review may itself raise an issue. In addition, the fees for the services may have changed or the extent of the services provided. Accordingly, each financial interest disclosed must be considered anew every year.

COMPONENTS OF THE CONFLICT-OF-INTEREST POLICY

Conflict-of-interest policies generally identify the individuals to be covered by the policy and the interests that must be disclosed, outline procedures to follow for the reporting and reviewing of conflicts, and provide guidance for documentation and disclosure. Some policies may also include examples of conflict situations. The sections that follow elaborate on the chief components of a conflict-of-interest policy, as shown in the sample provided in Appendix 3.

STATEMENT OF PURPOSE AND DUTIES OF OFFICERS AND DIRECTORS

The policy begins with a general statement of purpose and a brief description of the duties of loyalty and care that directors and officers owe to the organization. A conflict-of-interest policy is meant to protect both the organization and the board members, and should contain a statement to that effect.

It is important to remember that, if the IRS were to find a violation of either the intermediate sanctions rules or the private foundation self-dealing rules, a tax would be imposed on the person receiving the excess or impermissible benefit, and on directors and/or officers who knowingly approved the transaction. Additionally, a state attorney general could seek to penalize not only those involved in conflicts of interest, but other board members, and in some circumstances, could replace some or all board members who were found not to be doing their job by allowing such incidents to occur. Therefore, it is in every board member's interest to understand the organization's conflict policy and fulfill the required disclosure obligations.

It also is in all board members' best interests to be mindful of the "court of public opinion." Where conflict situations arise, there are few things more embarrassing to an organization or more likely to hurt its prospects or reputation, than professions of ignorance by uninvolved board members about problematic situations.

Direct or Indirect Financial, Competing, or Other Material Interest

This section of the policy describes in detail the types of interests that must be disclosed by individuals covered by the policy. Once disclosed, these interests must be reviewed by the board or the chosen committee, and must receive that body's disinterested approval — again, without the participation of the interested board member. The board must be sure that these transactions are favorable to the organization; in other words, no excess benefit is provided to the interested board member and there is no more advantageous option available that would not involve a conflict of interest. Depending on the nature of the transaction and the parties involved, the organization may need to analyze the proposed transaction under the intermediate sanctions rules. If those rules are applicable, the organization should take the necessary steps to obtain the rebuttable presumption of reasonableness as described in Chapter 3.

Generally, a director or officer must disclose a "direct or indirect financial, competing or other material interest" in a proposed or existing contract, transaction, or arrangement of the organization. What constitutes a direct or indirect financial, competing or other material interest is defined in some detail in the policy, and includes three different types of interests, discussed below. It may be helpful to review that section of the sample policy together with this discussion.

> *Type 1. A substantial financial interest or a competing interest directly in the proposed or existing contract or transaction.*

Type 1 Examples

The key here, of course, is what is meant by "substantial." The policy outlines three ways in which an interest will be considered substantial. The first involves the level of ownership in a public or private company doing business with the organization, and the policy sets forth percentage of ownership thresholds triggering the disclosure requirement. (For example, a charity's board member and his family are the owners of a printing company that is the principal provider of printing services to the charity for its direct mail production.) The second involves an ownership or investment interest in an entity doing business with the organization and that produces income for a director or officer that is significant to him or her. (For example, a school's director owns a small percentage of a public company's stock, but that stock represents more than half of her net worth and the public company provides telecommunication services to the school.) The third is a compensation arrangement with an entity or individual doing business with the organization. (For example, a volunteer director of a foundation is a highly compensated executive of an investment banking firm, but not an owner, and his firm manages part of the foundation's endowment.) The sample policy includes detailed descriptions of each of these substantial interests.

What happens in this regard if a board member is affiliated with the only vendor available to provide certain goods or services to the organization? This is often referred to as the "sole source" problem. The first responsibility of the organization is to confirm that this truly is the only available or reasonable source. In remote areas, for example, there may be few choices of service providers. Additionally, certain service providers may be unique in nature. The board then must fully understand the nature and extent of the board member's relationship to this vendor. The organization must also make sure that it is treated at least as favorably as other customers of that vendor. If the organization receives a fair price and the board member oversees the project and ensures superior performance and service, this could be helpful and of benefit to the organization.

This type of conflict situation may instead involve a competing interest. A board member has a competing interest if he or she would like to take advantage of a business opportunity that is being considered by the organization. If, for example, a board member is a developer and would like to purchase a parcel of land that he knows would be particularly beneficial for the organization because of its size and location, he must disclose to the organization both the opportunity and his interest in pursuing it.

> *Type 2. A substantial financial interest in any other organization that (a) is a party to the proposed or existing contract, transaction or arrangement; or (b) is in any way involved in the proposed or existing contract, transaction or arrangement, including through the provision of services in connection therewith; or (c) has a competing interest in the proposed or existing contract, transaction or arrangement.*

The first prong of this category of interest is most easily recognizable because it involves an interest in the entity doing business with the nonprofit organization. The second prong is aimed at identifying more indirect interests. The third deals with interests in entities that have competing interests.

Type 2 Example

Edna is a partner in the architectural firm of Brown & Miller and serves on the board of directors of Neighborhood Nonprofit. Brown & Miller provides architectural services to Neighborhood Nonprofit at a discounted rate. Edna has disclosed to the board the fact that Brown & Miller provides such architectural services and the rates that Brown & Miller charges. Now, Neighborhood Nonprofit is negotiating a major contract with a family-owned construction business. Brown & Miller regularly provides architectural services to that business and has been asked to provide its services in connection with the construction project that is under negotiation. Therefore, Edna has a substantial financial interest in an organization (the architectural firm) that will be "involved" in the transaction. Edna's firm will get additional business if that family-owned construction business is selected as the contractor for the project. Edna has a conflict of interest in the transaction because she has a financial interest that could impair her objectivity in voting on whether that contractor is selected and whether the project price is a fair one. Edna must disclose that interest to the board.

> *Type 3. Holds a position as trustee, director, officer, member, or employee in any party to the proposed or existing contract, transaction, or arrangement, or any organization that is in any way involved in the proposed contract, transaction, or arrangement, including through the provision of services in connection therewith, or any competing organization.*

This would include a situation where an individual's conflicting interest may not be a financial one.

Type 3 Examples

Susan serves on the boards of two nonprofit organizations that are considering a merger. If one of the organizations (Children's Charity) is floundering and may not survive if the merger does not take place and Susan has been involved in that organization since its formation, Susan has a strong interest in seeing it survive — although its survival will not provide the other organization (Care for Children) with any financial benefit. Susan may wish to vote for the merger even though Care for Children, the more successful flourishing nonprofit, has one or more other merger candidates that may bring more to it in terms of breadth of service, an attractive lease, or even something less tangible like reputational value. Although Susan has no financial interest, her role as a member of both boards may impair her objectivity with respect to the transaction.

This third interest category also covers a grantmaking situation commonly encountered by private foundations. For example, if a foundation board member also serves on the board of an organization seeking funds from the foundation, that affiliation must be disclosed and the board member should not advocate for the grant or vote on its approval. Of even greater concern would be if the board member were a staff member of the organization seeking a grant, particularly where the board member is directly involved in a project seeking funds. In this situation, the board member may, for example, be seeking to direct funds to a project, and his or her employment at the potential grantee organization may be affected by the continuation of that project, which in turn depends on the receipt of additional funding.

Foundations also frequently face situations where a board member seeks to direct funds to a relative, friend, or client or to an organization with which such an individual is associated. Foundations that make grants to individuals must be particularly careful in ensuring that any personal or financial relationship between a board member and potential grantee, directly or indirectly through an organization, is fully disclosed and examined with respect to any conflict of interest — including any potential violation of the self-dealing rules.

Again, in this third category there may be even trickier situations that might not be covered under the specific language of the policy, but that clearly implicate conflicting interests.

Steven is a partner in a management consulting firm and his firm provides consulting services to Save Our Cities on whose board he sits. Steven's firm provides its services at discount rates. Save Our Cities is considering entering into a major contract with a family-owned business. Steven's firm will not be involved in any way in this contract; however, Steven's firm provides personal financial services to one of the owners of the family business. Steven knows that this particular contract is very important to his firm's client (the individual business owner). In addition, the client is a very important one to Steven's firm — particularly to the senior partner who runs Steven's practice group. Steven has no interest in any organization that is a party to the contract or that provides services to a party to the contract because his firm does not provide management consulting services to the family-owned business. However, Steven clearly has a business interest in the outcome of the vote on the contract and, therefore, may have difficulty considering only the best interest of the organization. Steven's fellow board members should be made aware of his conflicting interest and Steven may choose not to vote on this contract.

Drafting a conflict-of-interest policy that would cover this last situation is difficult because it easily can produce more information than is useful, and may also raise privacy issues. Nevertheless, it is important to be aware of how these types of relationships can affect board members' conduct. Because interconnected business and nonprofit relationships can make disinterested decision making extremely difficult, the policy should provide some guidance on what to do when these types of situations arise. The policy could encourage board members to discuss these situations with the board chair or designated compliance officer, so that necessary disclosure is accomplished without board members feeling that they must relinquish all privacy.

What Happens When a Direct or Indirect Financial, Competing or Other Material Interest Is Reported?

The conflict-of-interest policy must also address what happens when a direct or indirect financial, competing or other material interest is reported. Once the required disclosure is made, it is not up to the individual with the conflicting interest to determine whether an impermissible conflict exists or how to address the conflicting interest. The compliance officer or committee responsible for reviewing disclosure statements and monitoring compliance with the policy evaluates the possible conflict, following the procedure outlined in the policy. The chosen compliance officer, as well as board members serving on the board committee charged with reviewing conflicts, must have a thorough enough understanding of the laws regulating conflicting interests in order to properly advise the full board, with the advice of legal counsel when necessary, as to whether such competing or conflicting interests could cause a legal and/or public relations issue for the organization.

Section 4 of the sample policy in Appendix 3 describes in detail what should happen at the board or committee meeting when a transaction is discussed in which a director or officer has disclosed an interest. Although the interested board member may answer questions and express an opinion about the proposed transaction, he or she should leave the meeting prior to the detailed discussion and actual decision making; to do otherwise would inhibit discussion of a sensitive issue and, perhaps, skew the outcome. The board or committee must make a determination (without the participation of the interested board member) as to whether the transaction at hand is the best one for the organization or if a more advantageous one may be available that would not give rise to a conflict of interest.

In this examination, the group must also determine whether the proposed transaction could constitute self-dealing in the case of a private foundation or be an excess benefit transaction if the organization is a public charity. If the proposed activity appears to be prohibited under one of these federal tax regimes, the board or committee should consult with legal counsel before approving the transaction.

If the board decides that the transaction or other matter involving a conflicting interest does not involve self-dealing in the case of a foundation or an excess benefit for other organizations, and no better option is available, it is free to approve the transaction being discussed. If, however, the board or other decision-making body decides that a better deal is available elsewhere, it should not approve the transaction. The existence of an alternative would eliminate any justification for proceeding with a transaction that would benefit a board member but would confer no advantage on the nonprofit organization.

Sufficient time to acquire additional information should be taken into account when acting on conflict matters. There will almost always be a need to develop information on alternatives and examine them. In determining whether a better arrangement is available, the board may consider qualitative as well as quantitative factors (for example, the best consultant or lawyer for a particular assignment may not be the one with the lowest fees).

Recording Reported Interests

Section 5 of the policy in Appendix 3 details the information that should be included in the meeting minutes. The following should be recorded: the names of individuals who disclosed or were otherwise found to have a direct or indirect financial, competing or other material interest in a proposed or existing contract or transaction of the organization; the nature of the interest; and the extent of the director's or officer's participation in the relevant board or committee meeting related to the possible conflict. The minutes should also include a record of any determination as to whether the arrangement was fair and reasonable to the organization, and the specific reasons supporting the final decision — including any alternatives to the proposed or existing arrangement, the names of the persons who were present for discussions relating to the arrangement, and a record of any votes taken in connection with the decision. Although board minutes generally should not contain an overly detailed account of discussions during a meeting, where a conflict is involved, an organization should consider including an account of the nature of the related discussion.

Co-Investment Interest

The sample policy includes a special section on co-investment interests because many nonprofit organizations are now facing this issue. Each person covered by the policy must disclose whether he or she, or a relative (as defined in the policy), has personal funds invested with an investment manager providing, or expecting to provide, investment management services to the organization or in a professionally managed investment fund in which the organization is invested or is considering investing. Disclosures of such interests should be made to the organization's finance committee or investment committee, as appropriate. (These interests are also important when evaluating an investment manager's performance. A board member involved in this kind of oversight decision may be affected by his own interests if he or a close family member retains the same manager.)

Because members of an organization's finance committee themselves may be in the investment management business, this is an area where additional conflicts may arise. For example, a member of a finance committee may encourage the organization to invest in a particular investment vehicle in which he has advised other clients to invest. He may have only the organization's best interest in mind and the investment may be a good one for the organization. On the other hand, the board member could have conflicting interests where a minimum investment is required to launch the investment and the organization's funds are needed to reach that minimum.

Failure to Disclose

The organization also must consider what action it will take with respect to a director or officer who fails to make the disclosures required by the conflict-of-interest policy. If an individual fails to disclose a conflicting interest, he threatens the disinterested decision-making process critical to the oversight function of the board. The disclosure requirement will not be effective if the organization does not enforce it. (See Chapter 5 for further discussion.)

The sample conflict-of-interest policy outlines a process for conducting an inquiry when a board member's failure to disclose becomes apparent, and this process is described in more detail in Chapter 5. These situations should be addressed as promptly as possible to stop a board member from advancing his or her own financial or other material interests at the expense of the organization he or she serves. The board must take action expeditiously and thoughtfully so that the organization's reputation is not tarnished by negative reports in the media or government investigations. Although it may be difficult to do, such situations should be addressed as collegially as possible to avoid polarizing the board and damaging board members' mutual trust even further.

THE DISCLOSURE STATEMENT

As discussed above in connection with the sample policy, the duty imposed on individuals covered by a conflict-of-interest policy is a duty of disclosure. Without a conflict policy, many board members are confused about what it is they need to disclose and when they are considered to have conflicting interests. Board members who may appreciate that some disclosure is necessary may not take the obligation seriously if the organization does not have a policy with specific disclosure obligations.

Some board members may feel that being asked to complete a conflict disclosure statement signals to them a sense of mistrust on the part of the organization to which they are donating their time and often their money. To offset this, the disclosure process should make clear to board members that the purpose of the conflict-of-interest policy and the disclosure statement is to protect both them and the organization by identifying potential conflict situations before they can become problematic, and not to intrude on their lives or "check up" on them.

An annual disclosure statement must be required to make a conflict-of-interest policy effective. Otherwise, the conflict policy will simply be just another of the many documents distributed to board members and either read and filed away, or possibly never read at all. Thus, the conflict-of-interest policy includes a disclosure statement that must be completed and returned by each person covered by the policy on an annual basis (please see Appendix 4 for a sample document). By signing the disclosure statement, an individual also agrees to promptly report any situation that comes up in the future and involves an interest that is required to be disclosed by the policy. This means that if a conflicting interest arises during the year, the individual must report it to the organization even if the annual disclosure statement is not yet due. All board members and staff people covered by the conflict-of-interest policy must review their disclosure statements once a year and amend them as necessary to ensure that they are current. In organizations where there are particular concerns about conflicting interests, board members may be given a copy of their disclosure statement for review and any needed amendments more often than once a year.

As shown in the sample, the disclosure statement should ask the individual board member or officer to confirm that he or she has read and is familiar with the policy and either (1) to state that he or she is not aware of any direct or indirect financial, competing or other material interest that is required to be disclosed, or (2) to indicate that he or she has such an interest and to provide a letter detailing the nature of the interest.

Disclosure statements may take other forms as well. Some organizations create a lengthy questionnaire to try to ferret out potential conflicts covered by the policy. Although some individuals may consider a questionnaire easy to complete, others are intimidated, annoyed, and/or confused by the lengthier form and, as a result, may not complete it at all. Cooperation by board members will vary from one organization to another, and boards have different cultures that will make one form of disclosure statement more productive than another. Because detailed questionnaires are very organization specific, a sample has not been included in the appendix, but this approach should be kept in mind as an option if the more general disclosure form is not effective.

Some organizations include in their policies examples of interests that are required to be disclosed under the policy. That may be helpful but it must be made clear that the examples are not meant to cover all situations requiring disclosure.

As stated earlier, every interest reported on a disclosure form should be reviewed anew, even if the same interest has been reported in prior years. The interest disclosed must be evaluated against the current facts of a transaction and the organization's current situation generally.

SPECIAL CONSIDERATIONS: FOUNDATIONS

As stated previously, the first inquiry for a private foundation is whether the conflicting interest constitutes prohibited self-dealing under the IRS rules. Accordingly, a private foundation's conflict policy should include a brief description of those rules similar to that included in Chapter 3. Upon disclosure, the conflicts committee or compliance officer should determine, with the advice of counsel, whether there is a self-dealing violation. Private foundations may wish to use a more detailed type of disclosure form with their board members and officers to prevent self-dealing.

Although grantmaking issues do not necessarily give rise to self-dealing, many foundations view disinterested grantmaking decisions as vital to their integrity and reputation. Therefore, foundations also may wish to specifically address grantmaking issues in the conflict-of-interest policy. Such a policy should provide guidelines on when the foundation will permit a grant to be made to an organization with which one of the foundation's directors or officers, or a family member of a director or officer, is affiliated. The affiliation may be as an officer, director, or employee of the grantee or a consultant to the grantee. The foundation's policies on the acceptability of such grants likely will depend on factors such as whether and to what extent the affiliated individual is involved in the development and/or implementation of the project being funded.

For example, the policy may specify that the foundation will not make a grant to support a project for which one of the board members carries immediate responsibility. The policy also may state that when a foundation makes a grant to an organization from which a director receives compensation, the foundation will specify that no part of the grant funds may be used to pay or to supplement the director's compensation.

This would not, however, prohibit a general support grant to an organization with which the director is affiliated, and many foundations believe it helpful to have a representative on the board of a grantee to monitor the grantee's progress in achieving the purposes of the grant.

Some foundations believe it helpful for a foundation representative to join the board of a potential grantee before the foundation makes a major donation to enable the foundation to learn more about the financial integrity and spending policies of the potential grantee.

SERVING A BROAD PURPOSE

Today, most individuals are likely to be uncomfortable serving on a nonprofit board that does not have a strictly enforced conflict-of-interest policy. No organization should take the unnecessary risk of not having a policy in place. Furthermore, given the increased attention to governance by regulators, watchdog groups, and donors, having and enforcing a conflict-of-interest policy will increasingly be expected of all nonprofit organizations and will ultimately lead to better decision making and reduced organizational risk. If an organization fails to have a policy, it will be much more difficult for a board member to demonstrate his or her claim of responsible behavior when it turns out that a fellow board member is making a substantial profit from work done for the organization. On the other hand, if the profiting board member completed a disclosure statement and failed to disclose the interest, then other board members are able to establish that they were actively misled.

Beyond this, members of nonprofit boards need to understand that creating and enforcing a conflict-of-interest policy is an essential part of fulfilling their duties to the organization they serve. Conflicts of interest have a way of stopping boards and entire organizations in their tracks. Taking a proactive approach to conflict-of-interest management can forestall many problems and keep the board — and the entire organization — focused on fulfilling the organization's mission.

CHAPTER 5

Addressing Conflicts of Interest after Problems Arise

By developing a conflict-of-interest policy and ensuring that all board members, officers, and relevant staff understand the policy and complete their disclosure statements, a nonprofit board can generally manage conflicts of interest so that they do not become problematic. However, the board must be prepared to address those situations when problems do occur.

These problems may happen due to an individual's failure to disclose a conflict of interest — either because a board member does not recognize the existence of a conflict or because he or she intentionally chooses not to disclose. The board may learn of the existence of a conflict at a board meeting where the transaction involving the conflict is being considered. It is also possible that the board may not uncover the existence of a conflict of interest until after the transaction has already been approved.

ESTABLISHING A PROCEDURE FOR RESPONDING

The best way to prepare for these situations is to establish a practice for responding to the reporting or discovery of a conflict of interest. Having an established procedure in place before problems occur will ensure that everyone on the board has a common understanding of what should happen in these difficult circumstances.

To encourage the disclosure of conflicts, it is critical that the organization carefully select whoever will serve as the compliance officer, and/or members of a conflicts committee, to ensure that the individuals are highly respected and approachable. If an individual compliance officer is selected, it is wise to also select an alternate in case the person reporting the conflict is not comfortable with the designated compliance officer, or if the compliance officer herself wishes to report a conflict.

If the conflict of interest is disclosed on an annual disclosure statement or is disclosed as soon as it is discovered and before a transaction is approved, then the procedures described in Chapter 4 should be followed. Again, the minutes of the board or committee meeting considering the transaction should state the nature of any conflicts that were disclosed and the names of those who disclosed the conflicting interests. The minutes should also reflect the decision as to whether or not the contract, transaction, or other arrangement being considered was found to be fair and reasonable and in the best interests of the organization. Any votes taken should be recorded in the minutes.

There will be occasions, however, where it may become apparent that a conflict of interest has not been disclosed. This might happen in a few different ways: A board member may realize that a conflict of interest has not been disclosed, either because it was overlooked or because new circumstances have created a situation that did not exist when he last updated the disclosure statement; a board member may perceive a conflict of interest in another colleague and raise a question with the compliance officer; or, the compliance officer himself may discover a conflict in connection with a transaction.

DISCUSSION WITH THE CONFLICTED BOARD MEMBER

If a board member realizes that he or she has not disclosed a conflict, either through inadvertence or because of new circumstances, the best first step is a discussion between the board member and the individual or group tasked with monitoring conflicts of interest. Who should attend this meeting will depend upon the particular relationships among board members; the goal is to have disinterested board members evaluating the conflict from the very beginning. If the organization has a conflicts committee, the meeting should include the members of the conflicts committee and the person with the conflict. If any members of the conflicts committee are not disinterested with respect to the conflict, then one or more other board members may need to be substituted. If an individual compliance officer is selected, the meeting should include the board member with the apparent conflict, the compliance officer, and the board chair (unless of course the board chair is the compliance officer, in which case another board member may be selected to participate, such as the chair of the governance committee). Again, the goal is to have at the meeting people who are objective and can evaluate the conflict fairly.

WHAT SHOULD BE DONE AFTER THE DISCUSSION?

If there is agreement on the nature of the conflict of interest and the actions that must be taken to rectify it, no further discussion is necessary. The proposed resolution should be presented to the board for approval.

It is possible, however, that the individual in question will not recognize the existence of a conflict of interest, even after conversations with the conflicts committee and/or compliance officer. If this is the case, and/or if those at the initial meeting are divided on the existence of a problematic conflict of interest, the matter should be taken to the full board.

Handling a Problem That Arises during a Board Meeting

Sometimes conflicts become apparent in the context of a board meeting and must be addressed there. How this is handled will depend on a number of factors, including the understanding and intentions of the person who has the conflict, as well as the nature of the conflict itself.

When a conflict becomes apparent at a board meeting, the person who recognizes it should make it known to the board chair. The board may then discuss the matter to identify possible courses of action. If the problem is related to the progress of the meeting itself, such as participation in a discussion or vote by someone who should have abstained, the error should be noted in the minutes and the vote retaken if necessary. The discussion should be recorded in the minutes of the meeting.

Discovery of Failure to Disclose

If someone other than the person with the conflict brings the problem to the compliance officer's attention, the situation may be a tricky one for the organization. The first danger is that a situation will develop where there is an "accuser" and an "accused," leading to the development of factions on the board where one group is supporting the person who apparently has a conflict and the other group is supporting the person who has identified it. This can cause irreparable harm to the organization. It is critical to make an effort to have the board work together to determine how best to address the conflict situation in the manner best suited to protect the organization as a whole.

In addition, if the board finds that an interested board member intentionally failed to disclose a conflict, or refuses to accept the existence of a conflict when presented to him or her, then the organization must determine what action to take with respect to the individual. Depending upon the nature of and the reasons for the individual's failure to disclose or recognize a conflict, the board may determine that he or she is not a productive board member for the organization and may choose not to re-elect him or her at the end of the term, or the board may seek to remove him or her from service immediately. Removal is, of course, a very serious step and should be taken only as a last resort — the board member being removed may challenge that action in court. In cases where an individual's action has harmed the organization, an action for damages may need to be brought against the board member to repair the organization.

Perhaps the most difficult type of conflict-of-interest situation for a board to handle is one involving the organization's founder. The sense of ownership that many founders have with regard to "their" organization may make it difficult to recognize or be willing to acknowledge that they may be seeking to use the assets of the organization in a way that would confer an improper financial benefit on themselves or on one of their relatives.

If a conflicting interest is not discovered until after a transaction is approved, the transaction may result in an act of self-dealing or an excess benefit transaction. If it does, the organization is required to report the transaction to the IRS in connection with the filing of its annual information return. As discussed previously, this may result in the imposition of taxes upon the individual who benefited from the transaction and failed to make the disclosure. If a tax is imposed, the transaction also will need to be corrected.

Having a clear protocol on how to deal with conflicts of interest will be invaluable for the compliance officer as well as for the full board. In this way, no one will be forced to rely on dim memories of what happened last time. Rather, board members will be able to proceed smoothly through a course of action that is equitable because it is the same for everyone, following procedures that take personal opinions and preferences out of the discussion.

CHAPTER 6
Conflicts of Interest and Ethical Considerations

Because nonprofit organizations are accountable to the public, many feel it important to do more than the minimum required to comply with legal conflict requirements; they wish to avoid, to the extent possible, even the appearance of a conflict of interest. The previous chapters addressed conflicts of interest that could expose the organization to legal penalties and/or regulatory scrutiny. Board members should also be aware of conflict situations that could damage an organization's public image and adversely affect its public support. Donors and volunteers set high standards and will be more likely to give of their time and support to an organization where they believe board members, officers, and employees act in an honest and ethical manner. At the same time, the working environment for volunteers and staff alike will be far more collegial and generally free of conflict if everyone at the organization is expected to act in an open and honest manner and to treat colleagues as well as donors, volunteers, and members of the community with respect.

ORGANIZATIONAL CODE OF ETHICS

Many nonprofit organizations concerned with ethical conduct are developing separate policies in that regard, setting forth the organization's mission, the ideals of behavior that the organization expects from volunteers and staff, and a process for reporting improper conduct by others. These codes of ethics are very different from conflict-of-interest policies — they are intended to guide behavior and decision making in a wide range of situations, and they focus on general standards of conduct. Conflict-of-interest policies are more narrowly focused on identifying conflicts of interest and creating a procedure for managing them. Codes of ethics vary greatly from one organization to another, but generally reflect the following:

1. They are broad in scope, covering a variety of topics relating to institutional behavior.

2. They often discuss the mission of the organization and may also include a statement of organizational philosophy.

3. They often include provisions that are specific to the organization's mission. Hospitals, for example, may include a patient's bill of rights in their ethical codes. Medical associations may include standards of behavior that relate to their members, such as treatment of research subjects.

4. They set ethical standards for the organization as a whole, rather than covering only board members, officers, and senior staff.

5. They provide general guidelines for conduct, focusing on the shared dedication to a common mission and the importance of treating others at the organization with dignity and respect.

DEVELOPING A WRITTEN POLICY

Appendix 5 provides a sample policy for the promotion of ethical conduct for board members and staff alike. This ethical conduct policy states that the directors, officers, and staff of the organization are expected to maintain the highest standards of conduct and not simply to avoid potential legal sanctions. A special point is made in the ethical conduct policy regarding the relationship between board members and staff to address concerns that board members expect the staff to serve them personally rather than treating them as colleagues jointly pursuing the organization's charitable mission.

It is important to include in the ethical conduct policy a procedure for the reporting of questionable conduct. In the sample included in Appendix 5, board members are directed to raise concerns with the chair or treasurer of the board. Employees are to contact their supervisor or the director of human resources. The ethical conduct policy also addresses who will make determinations with respect to reports of unethical conduct. The sample policy assigns this responsibility to the board. Alternatively, the board could delegate the responsibility to a board committee, such as the executive committee or governance committee.

With respect to employees, codes of conduct also may be contained in the organization's employee handbook.

CREATING A CULTURE OF INTEGRITY

Boards that do not choose to develop a written ethical conduct policy still benefit from taking the time to define the organization's values and think about the implications of those values for board member and staff behavior. Consideration of the broader ethical context is especially useful in situations that involve a potential or perceived conflict rather than one that is clearly defined by law. Frank and open discussions of integrity and responsibility can help board members understand public perceptions of their actions and decisions, and successfully address situations that could present apparent conflicts of interest. These discussions also remind board members to think about fostering ethical conduct to create an atmosphere and culture of integrity throughout the organization.

Board members and senior staff should be leaders in defining and promoting that culture within the organization and in interactions with the organization's stakeholders. A code of ethics is best used to engender this organizational culture; if ethical behavior is valued throughout the organization, it likely will make it more difficult for individuals to act purely out of self-interest.

Neither the code of ethics nor the conflict-of-interest policy is designed to cover every possible situation and occurrence. However, the organization can use the two policies together to help prevent problematic conflicts and effectively manage conflicts of all types, and that fall on all points on the continuum.

CHAPTER 7
Whistleblower Policy

The Sarbanes-Oxley Act requires that nonprofit organizations provide protection for whistleblowers and imposes penalties for actions against them. In response to this requirement, organizations are strongly encouraged to adopt a whistleblower policy to ensure compliance and to provide a means for employees, officers, and directors to raise good-faith concerns about behavior that appears to be illegal, dishonest, or unethical. A sample Whistleblower Policy is included in Appendix 6.

The IRS Form 990 asks specifically whether the organization has a written whistleblower policy and it is preferable to be able to answer yes to that question.

The bill introduced in May 2012 at the request of the New York State Attorney General discussed in Chapter 1 includes a requirement that every corporation that has five or more employees and in the prior fiscal year had annual revenue in excess of one million dollars shall adopt a whistleblower policy to protect from retaliation persons who report suspected improper conduct.[31] The policy must provide that no director, officer, employee, or volunteer who in good faith reports any action or suspected action taken by or within the corporation that is illegal, fraudulent, or in violation of any adopted policy of the corporation shall suffer intimidation, harassment, discrimination, or other retaliation or, in the case of an employee, adverse employment consequences. The bill lists provisions that must be in the policy including

1. procedures for reporting, handling and investigating violations or suspected violations of laws or corporate policies, including procedures for maintaining confidentiality

2. a requirement that an employee of the corporation be designated to administer, implement, and oversee compliance of the whistleblower policy, and to report to the audit committee or other committee of independent directors or, if there are no such committees, to the board

---

[31] S. 7431, 235th Sess. (N.Y. 2011).

3. a provision regarding retention of documents for at least six years

4. a requirement that the policy be distributed to all directors, officers, employees and volunteers, with instructions

While this bill was not enacted during the 2012 Legislative Session, it is expected that the bill, or a modified version thereof, will be re-introduced during the 2013 Legislative Session.

CONTENTS OF THE POLICY

The whistleblower policy should cover all employees, officers and directors and should provide examples of the types of serious misconduct covered by the policy. The sample policy in Appendix 6 includes a list of examples.

Careful consideration should be given to who shall serve as the compliance officer under the whistleblower policy so as not to discourage reporting.

Two compliance officers may be chosen. If the compliance officer or officers are staff members, the policy should provide for alternative reporting if the whistleblower is uncomfortable communicating his concerns to the compliance officers or is unsatisfied with the response. This could include reporting to the chair of the board or other board member. This is necessary, in particular, if the complaint involves the chief executive or other senior executive.

The policy also should state that allegations may be reported anonymously. Upon receipt of a complaint, the compliance officer must advise the president, chair of the board, treasurer or other designated board member.

Some organizations use an outside company to provide a 24 hour, 7 day a week hotline for employees who are not comfortable with reporting a complaint to an internal compliance officer. In this way, the whistleblower is not required to give his name and is not required to speak to someone he knows. He is given a number for identification purposes. The information then is relayed to the organization's management. The whistleblower may be given a date to call back for follow-up and to provide any additional information requested by the organization's management.

Regardless of the identity of the compliance officers, there is no reporting back to the whistleblower on the progress of the investigation. The whistleblower is not a partner in the investigative process.

A key component of the policy is the prohibition on retaliation against anyone who makes a good-faith allegation under the policy. In that regard, the policy should provide that any person who retaliates against a whistleblower will be subject to disciplinary action, including possible termination in the case of an employee.

The policy should set forth the procedures for investigating the complaint and should make clear that the compliance officer is not required to investigate broad, nonspecific allegations. To discourage the reporting of knowingly false allegations, the policy should provide that any employee, officer, or director who knowingly makes a false allegation with malicious intent or knowingly produces false information in connection with a complaint will be subject to disciplinary measures.

CONCLUSION

Every nonprofit organization should have in place a means of identifying and managing conflicting interests. The heightened concern of the public, the demands of funders and donors, and the interest of the IRS and state attorneys general make a written conflict-of-interest policy a virtual requirement for almost all nonprofit organizations today. In fact, it is difficult to imagine a nonprofit entity that would not benefit from having a conflict-of-interest policy.

Nonprofit boards should use the process of developing the policy as a way of strengthening their ability to support their organizations and promote organizational missions and goals. By giving careful attention to conflict-of-interest matters, a nonprofit board can ensure that all board members recognize conflicts of interest and understand the circumstances under which they can be legally problematic or can cause public relations issues. As discussed in Chapter 6, many organizations also find it useful to focus on the ethical considerations involved in the conduct of both board and staff members to help instill a culture of honesty and loyalty in the organization.

Service on a nonprofit board can be profoundly satisfying on a variety of emotional and intellectual levels, especially when board members know that they are fulfilling their duties of care, loyalty, and obedience to the best of their abilities. Board service is most gratifying when board members are able to focus on achieving the organization's mission. This can happen safely only when a board member understands when he or she may have a conflict of interest, when conflicting interests must be disclosed, and how the organization will manage and respond. Having a living conflict-of-interest policy that adequately produces such disclosure is a key part of an organization's overall process for managing conflicting interests.

APPENDIX 1

Q&As

1. **Is there a conflict of interest if a board member volunteers her skills and advice in her field of expertise to the organization she serves?**

   The effectiveness of a board of directors depends largely on the participation of individuals who have a variety of talents and experiences in areas such as finance, development, public relations, and law, as well as expertise in the substantive area that is the focus of the organization's mission. Doctors and scientists, for example, add enormous value to boards and advisory groups of scientific research and medical organizations. As long as these individuals have no direct or indirect or other material interest in a particular transaction or arrangement as described in detail in Chapter 4, they can and should use their knowledge and skills to guide the organization. An expert in strategic planning who serves as a board member can be a great resource for the organization in its strategic planning process. Similarly, an executive recruiter can chair a transition committee leading the search for a new chief financial officer, and an events planner can provide input to staff on organizing an annual benefit.

   When a board member shares her expertise with the organization at no charge and is not using the work she does for the organization — or confidential information she obtains — as a means of advancing her own business interest, she is simply acting as a valuable board member and no conflict of interest will arise.

   The organization must be satisfied, however, that the individual volunteering skills has the qualifications to do so and meets the organization's standards. To avoid a problem — akin to a conflict — the organization must be free to accept or reject any such offer.

2. **If the chief executive works with an executive coach whom she believes has been helpful to her, does it present any problems for the organization if the chief executive brings that executive coach in to work with the organization's staff and also the organization's board members?**

   This situation is fraught with potential conflicts. Is the chief executive doing what he believes is best for the organization? Or has the executive coach been asking for an opportunity to come in and work with the staff and board of the organization and the chief executive agrees so as not to jeopardize the working relationship with the coach? What if the coach's advice is not helpful to the organization? Will the chief executive be able to evaluate the coach's services objectively? Will he be hesitant to criticize the coach or terminate his services if that is the appropriate action to take? Additionally, the same person who is knowledgeable on coaching staff members may not have the requisite knowledge and experience to advise nonprofit board members on what their role and responsibilities are. Moreover, the executive coach who has been working with the chief executive may be in a difficult position, owing loyalty to the chief executive who is a former and perhaps current client and, at the same time, coaching the board, particularly with respect to the role of the board in monitoring the chief executive. The coach may downplay problems that may arise with the chief executive, particularly if the chief executive's actions reflect reliance on the coach's advice.

3. **Is there a conflict if a board member asks the chief executive to serve on the board of an organization for which the board member serves as chief executive?**

   This situation is not advisable. It opens up the real potential for each of these individuals to act for the benefit of the other with the implied understanding that the favor will be returned. This is the type of situation that raises the concerns of regulators and could give rise to precisely the type of joint approval arrangement that the IRS views as interfering with independent decision making. As noted in Chapter 3 regarding the safe harbor under the intermediate sanctions rules, a compensation arrangement or other transaction between an organization and a disqualified person must be approved by an independent authorized body. The intermediate sanctions rules provide that a joint approval arrangement, whereby an individual approves compensation of the disqualified person and the disqualified person, in turn, approves that individual's compensation or a transaction providing economic benefits to such individual, does not satisfy the independence requirement.

4. **Is there a conflict of interest if an organization's clients serve on the board?**

Representatives from an organization's clients can be valuable board members because they help ensure that the board is aware of and responsive to the needs of those the organization was formed to serve. "Constituent" board members must be aware, however, that they naturally have dual interests. For example, parents who serve on the board of an independent school have the interests of their child in mind as well as those of the school. With respect to improvements in the quality of education provided, those interests converge. If the board is voting on a tuition increase that the school believes it needs but the parents can ill afford, then the parents may have difficulty casting their votes in the best interests of the school. That is true as well when a school that serves elementary and middle school children is considering expanding to open a high school. Parents whose children will otherwise age out of the school may be in favor of adding a high school even if it does not appear to be the best financial choice for the school. In such case, the best approach may be for the parents not to participate in the vote.

Similarly, if physicians serve on a hospital board, they may have an interest in expanding the departments in their own specialties even if those are not the most profitable areas for the hospital.

5. **What policies should be followed where a relative of the chief executive is hired by the organization?**

Where a relative of the chief executive is particularly qualified for a position at the organization, hiring him may be in the best interest of the organization. For example, an organization that works in a public housing community may have difficulty in obtaining and keeping employees due to violence. Suppose the son of the organization's chief executive has experience working with at risk youth and the organization's development director has worked directly with this young man and knows him to be particularly able. The development director recommends the chief executive's son for the job based on the development director's knowledge of and personal experience with the young man's work.

First, the organization should be able to show how this young man's skills and experience are well suited to the open position and why he would benefit the organization. Otherwise, all employees would question why their children or relatives are not given positions at the organization. That is particularly true where the potential employee is the child of the chief executive, although here, of course, many parents may not wish to have their children in what may be considered to be a dangerous position.

If the organization does hire one or more relatives of current employees, the organization will benefit from adopting a nepotism policy. Such policy could provide, for example, that one relative may not be in a position to influence the work responsibilities, salary, hours, career progress, benefits or other terms and conditions of employment of the other relative without specific approval and oversight of a board committee such as the compensation committee or governance committee. The policy should also provide a procedure for addressing complaints by an employee who believes he or she has been treated unfairly as a result of having a relative employed at the organization.

6. **Is there a conflict of interest if the organization's auditors provide other services to the organization?**

Technically, such an arrangement does not create a conflict of interest because the auditors are neither officers, directors, nor other disqualified persons relative to the organization. However, arrangements where an organization's auditors provide consulting or other services to an audit client may impair the integrity of the vital audit function. This is why the Sarbanes-Oxley Act prohibits auditing firms for publicly traded companies from providing nonaudit services — with the exception of tax services — to audit clients. Although not applicable to nonprofits, this provision of Sarbanes-Oxley is one that nonprofits would be wise to adopt. In other words, nonprofit organizations should look to their auditors primarily for audit and tax services, such as preparing the IRS Form 990 or 990-PF.

APPENDIX 2

IRS Form 1023 Requirements, Instructions, and Sample IRS Conflict-of-Interest Policy

Part V of the IRS Form 1023 covers Compensation and Other Financial Arrangements with Your Officers, Directors, Trustees, Employees, and Independent Contractors. Line 5 of this section asks three questions about the applicant organization's procedures for handling conflicts of interest:

> 5a. Have you adopted a conflict-of-interest policy consistent with the sample conflict-of-interest policy in Appendix A to the instructions? If "Yes," provide a copy of the policy and explain how the policy has been adopted, such as by resolution of your governing board. If "No," answer lines 5b and 5c.

> 5b. What procedures will you follow to assure that persons who have a conflict of interest will not have influence over you for setting their own compensation?

> 5c. What procedures will you follow to assure that persons who have a conflict of interest will not have influence over you regarding business deals with themselves?

Note: A conflict-of-interest policy is recommended though it is not required to obtain exemption.

The instructions for line 5a state:

A "conflict of interest" arises when a person in a position of authority over an organization, such as a director, officer, or manager, may benefit personally from a decision he or she could make. Adoption of a conflict-of-interest policy is not required to obtain tax-exempt status. However, by adopting the sample policy or a similar policy, you will be choosing to put in place procedures that will help you avoid the possibility that those in positions of authority over you may receive an inappropriate benefit.

SAMPLE IRS CONFLICT-OF-INTEREST POLICY

Note: Items marked *Hospital Insert — for hospitals that complete Schedule C* are intended to be adopted by hospitals.

ARTICLE I: PURPOSE

The purpose of the conflict-of-interest policy is to protect this tax-exempt organization's (Organization) interest when it is contemplating entering into a transaction or arrangement that might benefit the private interest of an officer or director of the Organization or might result in a possible excess benefit transaction. This policy is intended to supplement but not replace any applicable state and federal laws governing conflict of interest applicable to nonprofit and charitable organizations.

ARTICLE II: DEFINITIONS

1. Interested Person

Any director, principal officer, or member of a committee with governing board delegated powers, who has a direct or indirect financial interest, as defined below, is an interested person.

[Hospital Insert — for hospitals that complete Schedule C

If a person is an interested person with respect to any entity in the health care system of which the organization is a part, he or she is an interested person with respect to all entities in the health care system.]

2. Financial Interest

A person has a financial interest if the person has, directly or indirectly, through business, investment, or family:

(a) An ownership or investment interest in any entity with which the Organization has a transaction or arrangement,

(b) A compensation arrangement with the Organization or with any entity or individual with which the Organization has a transaction or arrangement, or

(c) A potential ownership or investment interest in, or compensation arrangement with, any entity or individual with which the Organization is negotiating a transaction or arrangement.

Compensation includes direct and indirect remuneration as well as gifts or favors that are not insubstantial.

A financial interest is not necessarily a conflict of interest. Under Article III, Section 2, a person who has a financial interest may have a conflict of interest only if the appropriate governing board or committee decides that a conflict of interest exists.

ARTICLE III: PROCEDURES

1. Duty to Disclose

In connection with any actual or possible conflict of interest, an interested person must disclose the existence of the financial interest and be given the opportunity to disclose all material facts to the directors and members of committees with governing board delegated powers considering the proposed transaction or arrangement.

2. Determining Whether a Conflict of Interest Exists

After disclosure of the financial interest and all material facts, and after any discussion with the interested person, he/she shall leave the governing board or committee meeting while the determination of a conflict of interest is discussed and voted upon. The remaining board or committee members shall decide if a conflict of interest exists.

3. Procedures for Addressing the Conflict of Interest

(a) An interested person may make a presentation at the governing board or committee meeting, but after the presentation, he/she shall leave the meeting during the discussion of, and the vote on, the transaction or arrangement involving the possible conflict of interest.

(b) The chairperson of the governing board or committee shall, if appropriate, appoint a disinterested person or committee to investigate alternatives to the proposed transaction or arrangement.

(c) After exercising due diligence, the governing board or committee shall determine whether the Organization can obtain with reasonable efforts a more advantageous transaction or arrangement from a person or entity that would not give rise to a conflict of interest.

(d) If a more advantageous transaction or arrangement is not reasonably possible under circumstances not producing a conflict of interest, the governing board or committee shall determine by a majority vote of the disinterested directors whether the transaction or arrangement is in the Organization's best interest, for its own benefit, and whether it is fair and reasonable. In conformity with the above determination it shall make its decision as to whether to enter into the transaction or arrangement.

4. **Violations of the Conflicts-of-Interest Policy**

   (a) If the governing board or committee has reasonable cause to believe a member has failed to disclose actual or possible conflicts of interest, it shall inform the member of the basis for such belief and afford the member an opportunity to explain the alleged failure to disclose.

   (b) If, after hearing the member's response and after making further investigation as warranted by the circumstances, the governing board or committee determines the member has failed to disclose an actual or possible conflict of interest, it shall take appropriate disciplinary and corrective action.

ARTICLE IV: RECORDS OF PROCEEDINGS

The minutes of the governing board and all committees with board delegated powers shall contain:

   (a) The names of the persons who disclosed or otherwise were found to have a financial interest in connection with an actual or possible conflict of interest, the nature of the financial interest, any action taken to determine whether a conflict of interest was present, and the governing board's or committee's decision as to whether a conflict of interest in fact existed.

   (b) The names of the persons who were present for discussions and votes relating to the transaction or arrangement, the content of the discussion, including any alternatives to the proposed transaction or arrangement, and a record of any votes taken in connection with the proceedings.

ARTICLE V: COMPENSATION

   (a) A voting member of the governing board who receives compensation, directly or indirectly, from the Organization for services is precluded from voting on matters pertaining to that member's compensation.

   (b) A voting member of any committee whose jurisdiction includes compensation matters and who receives compensation, directly or indirectly, from the Organization for services is precluded from voting on matters pertaining to that member's compensation.

   (c) No voting member of the governing board or any committee whose jurisdiction includes compensation matters and who receives compensation, directly or indirectly, from the Organization, either individually or collectively, is prohibited from providing information to any committee regarding compensation.

[Hospital Insert — for hospitals that complete Schedule C

(d) Physicians who receive compensation from the Organization, whether directly or indirectly or as employees or independent contractors, are precluded from membership on any committee whose jurisdiction includes compensation matters. No physician, either individually or collectively, is prohibited from providing information to any committee regarding physician compensation.]

ARTICLE VI: ANNUAL STATEMENTS

Each director, principal officer, and member of a committee with governing board delegated powers shall annually sign a statement that affirms such person:

(a) Has received a copy of the conflicts-of-interest policy,

(b) Has read and understands the policy,

(c) Has agreed to comply with the policy, and

(d) Understands the Organization is charitable and in order to maintain its federal tax exemption it must engage primarily in activities which accomplish one or more of its tax-exempt purposes.

ARTICLE VII: PERIODIC REVIEWS

To ensure the Organization operates in a manner consistent with charitable purposes and does not engage in activities that could jeopardize its tax-exempt status, periodic reviews shall be conducted. The periodic reviews shall, at a minimum, include the following subjects:

(a) Whether compensation arrangements and benefits are reasonable, based on competent survey information, and the result of arm's length bargaining.

(b) Whether partnerships, joint ventures, and arrangements with management organizations conform to the Organization's written policies, are properly recorded, reflect reasonable investment or payments for goods and services, further charitable purposes, and do not result in inurement, impermissible private benefit, or in an excess benefit transaction.

ARTICLE VIII: USE OF OUTSIDE EXPERTS

When conducting the periodic reviews as provided for in Article VII, the Organization may, but need not, use outside advisors. If outside experts are used, their use shall not relieve the governing board of its responsibility for ensuring periodic reviews are conducted.

APPENDIX 3

Sample Conflict-of-Interest Policy

PURPOSE OF POLICY AND DUTIES OF DIRECTORS AND OFFICERS

The Directors and Officers of [Name of Organization] (["organization acronym"] or the "Organization") owe a duty of loyalty to the Organization, which requires that in serving the Organization they act, not in their personal interests or in the interests of others, but rather solely in the interests of the Organization. Directors and Officers must have an undivided allegiance to the Organization's mission and may not use their position as Directors or Officers, information they have about the Organization, or the Organization's property, in a manner that allows them to secure a pecuniary or other material benefit for themselves or their relatives.[1] Accordingly, no Director or Officer may use his or her position at the Organization for personal gain or to benefit another at the expense of the Organization, its mission, or its reputation.

A conflict of interest may arise when a person has an existing or potential financial interest or other material interest that impairs, or might appear to impair, his or her independence or objectivity in the discharge of responsibilities and duties to the Organization. This Policy is intended to protect the Organization's interests when it is contemplating entering into a contract, transaction, or arrangement that might benefit the private interests of a member of the Organization's Board of Directors or an Officer of the Organization.[2] This Policy is also meant to aid Directors and Officers of the Organization in performing the duties imposed upon them by the laws of the State of _____ and the United States of America with respect to their management responsibilities and fiduciary obligations to the Organization. The Organization is committed to transparency and openness in its operations.

Every Director and Officer must discharge his or her duties in good faith, with the degree of care that an ordinarily prudent person in a like position would exercise under similar circumstances. This requires using common sense, being diligent and attentive to the Organization's needs, and making thoughtful decisions in the best

---

[1]   For the purposes of this Policy, relative means spouse or significant other living in the same household ("partner"), siblings, partners of siblings, ancestors, children, grandchildren, great-grandchildren and partners of children, grandchildren, and great-grandchildren.

[2]   This Policy also applies to employees identified in Section 8.

interest of the Organization. No Director or Officer may take personal advantage of a business opportunity that is offered to the Organization unless the Board of Directors of the Organization first determines not to pursue such opportunity.

Each Director or Officer must protect the confidential information of the Organization and must not use confidential information of the Organization for his or her personal benefit, or use such confidential information or his or her position as a Director or Officer to the detriment of the Organization. Confidential information is information obtained through the Director's or Officer's position that has not become public information.

DIRECT OR INDIRECT FINANCIAL, COMPETING OR OTHER MATERIAL INTEREST

1. Contracts, transactions, or arrangements of the Organization in which a Director or Officer has a direct or indirect financial, competing, or other material interest shall not be prohibited, but they must be disclosed and they shall be subject to scrutiny. Any such proposed contract, transaction, or arrangement (collectively, "Arrangement") is to be reviewed to determine that it is in the best interests of the Organization.

2. For the purposes of this Policy, a Director or Officer has a direct or indirect financial, competing or other material interest in a proposed or existing Arrangement (a "Material Interest") if he or she, or one of his or her relatives:

   (a) has a substantial financial interest or a competing interest directly in the proposed or existing Arrangement; or

   (b) has a substantial financial interest in any other organization that i) is a party to the proposed or existing Arrangement; or ii) is in any way involved in the proposed or existing Arrangement, including through the provision of services in connection therewith (an "involved organization"); or iii) has a competing interest in the proposed or existing arrangement (a "competing organization"); or

   (c) holds a position as trustee, director, officer, member, partner, or employee in any party to the proposed or existing Arrangement or any involved or competing organization.

A Director's or Officer's interest will be considered to be a competing interest if the Director or Officer would like to take advantage of an opportunity in which the Organization also has an interest.

A Director's or Officer's financial interest will be considered substantial if it involves:

(a) an ownership or investment interest representing more than 1% of the outstanding shares of a publicly traded company or 5% of the outstanding shares or comparable interest of a privately owned company with which the Organization has or is negotiating an Arrangement or which is an involved or competing organization with respect to the Arrangement; or

(b) an ownership or investment interest, which produces a significant amount of income for or constitutes a significant part of the net worth of the Director or Officer, or a relative of the Director or Officer, in any entity with which the Organization has or is negotiating an Arrangement or which is an involved or competing organization with respect to the Arrangement; or

(c) a compensation arrangement of any kind with any entity or individual with which the Organization has or is negotiating an Arrangement or with any involved or competing organization with respect to the Arrangement.

DISCLOSURE OF INTEREST AND PARTICIPATION IN MEETING

3. Each Director and each Officer of the Organization shall promptly disclose any Material Interest that he or she has or reasonably expects to have in any proposed or existing Arrangement with the Organization prior to the start of any negotiations with respect to such matter. An interest required to be disclosed under this Policy shall be disclosed in writing to the Chairperson of the Board. Such disclosure shall include all material facts and supply any reasons why the Arrangement might be or not be in the best interest of the Organization. The Chairperson of the Board shall refer the issue to the full Board, the Executive Committee, or other Board Committee having decision-making authority over the substantive matter in question (the "Board or Committee").

4. The Director or Officer who discloses an interest in a proposed or existing Arrangement may make a presentation and respond to questions by the Board or Committee, but after such presentation, he or she shall leave the meeting during the discussion of, and vote on, the Arrangement that results in the conflict of interest. As part of any such presentation, the Director or Officer shall provide to the Board or Committee any reasons why the Arrangement might be or not be in the best interest of the Organization. The Board or Committee shall determine whether the Organization can obtain a more advantageous Arrangement with reasonable efforts from a person or entity that would not give rise to a conflict of interest. The Board or Committee shall, if appropriate, appoint a disinterested person or committee to

investigate alternatives to the proposed Arrangement. If a more advantageous contract, transaction, or arrangement is not reasonably attainable under circumstances that would not give rise to a conflict of interest, the Board or Committee shall determine by majority vote of the disinterested members of the Board or Committee whether the Arrangement is in the Organization's best interest and whether it is fair and reasonable to the Organization and shall make its decision as to whether to enter into the Arrangement in conformity with such determination.

MINUTES OF MEETING

5. The names of the Directors and Officers who disclosed or otherwise were found to have a Material Interest in a proposed or existing Arrangement of the Organization, the nature of the interest, and the extent of the Director's or Officer's participation in the relevant Board or Committee meeting on matters related to the Material Interest. The minutes also shall include a record of any determination as to whether the Arrangement was in the best interest of and fair and reasonable to the Organization, notwithstanding the interest, and the specific reasons supporting the determination, including any alternatives to the proposed or existing Arrangement, the names of the persons who were present for discussions and votes relating to the proposed or existing Arrangement, and a record of any votes taken in connection therewith.

CO-INVESTMENT INTEREST

6. Each Director and each Officer of the Organization also shall disclose whether he or she, or one of his or her relatives, has personal funds invested with an investment manager providing, or expected to provide, investment management services to the Organization or in a professionally managed investment fund in which the Organization is invested or is considering investing (a "Co-investment Interest"). For the purposes of this Conflicts Policy, a "professionally managed investment fund" shall not include mutual funds or other similar investment vehicles generally available to the investing public on essentially the same terms. Such Co-investment Interest shall be disclosed in writing to the Chairperson of the Board. Such disclosure shall include all material facts, including, but not limited to, fee arrangements and any preferential treatment received by the Director or Officer, or one of his or her relatives, and not available to other investors necessary to determine whether such Co-investment Interest may provide a benefit to the Director or Officer, or one of his or her relatives. If the Chairperson of the Board determines that the Co-investment Interest may provide some advantage to the Director or Officer, or one of his or her relatives, the

Chairperson of the Board shall refer the issue to the Organization's full Board of Directors or Investment Committee. The Director or Officer who discloses a Co-investment Interest may make a presentation and respond to questions from the Board of Directors or Investment Committee but shall not be present during the discussion of, and vote on, how to address the Co-investment Interest. The Board of Directors or the Investment Committee shall determine what, if any, corrective action is required with respect to the Co-investment Interest, including, but not limited to, terminating the investment relationship or seeking an adjustment in fee structure.

FAILURE TO DISCLOSE

7. If the Board or Committee has reasonable cause to believe that a Director or Officer has failed to disclose a Material Interest or Co-investment Interest subject to this Policy, it shall inform the Director or Officer of the basis for such belief and afford the Director or Officer an opportunity to explain the alleged failure to disclose. If, after hearing the response of such individual and making such further investigation as may be warranted in the circumstances, the Board or Committee determines that the Director or Officer has in fact failed to disclose a Material Interest or Co-investment Interest subject to this Policy, it shall take appropriate disciplinary and corrective action.

EMPLOYEES COVERED BY POLICY

8. This Policy shall apply to the Chief Executive Officer, the Chief Operating Officer, and the Chief Financial Officer.

ANNUAL DISCLOSURE STATEMENT

9. Each Director and Officer has a duty to place the interest of the Organization foremost in any dealing with the Organization and has a continuing responsibility to comply with the requirements of this Policy. Promptly following the adoption of this Policy, and thereafter not later than the first day of _____ of each year, each Director and Officer shall acknowledge his or her familiarity with this Policy and shall disclose in writing to the Chairperson of the Board any existing Material Interest or Co-investment Interest subject to this Policy by completing a Conflict-of-Interest Disclosure Statement. The Conflict-of-Interest Disclosure Statements shall be reviewed by the Chairperson of the Board. Any issues not previously disclosed shall be referred by him or her to the Board or appropriate Committee. The Conflict-of-Interest Disclosure Statements shall be retained in the confidential files of the Chair of the Board.

POLICY SUPPLEMENTS APPLICABLE LAWS

10. This Policy is intended to supplement but not replace any applicable state or federal laws governing conflicts of interest applicable to nonprofit charitable corporations.

APPENDIX 4

Sample Conflict-of-Interest Disclosure Statement

The Conflict-of-Interest Policy of the Organization requires any Director or Officer of the Organization to disclose any direct or indirect financial, competing or other material interest or co-investment interest that he or she has or reasonably expects to have in any proposed or existing contract, transaction, or arrangement with the Organization, or in any other matter under consideration or to be considered by the Board of Directors, the Executive Committee, or any other Board Committee.

Please initial each statement that applies to you:

_____ I have read and am familiar with the Conflict-of-Interest Policy.

_____ I am not aware of any direct or indirect financial, competing or other material interest or co-investment interest that is required to be disclosed under the Conflict-of-Interest Policy.

_____ I have described in the attached letter every direct or indirect financial, competing or other material interest or co-investment interest that is required to be disclosed under the Conflict-of-Interest Policy. (Please attach a letter providing complete details of any direct or indirect financial, competing or other material interest or co-investment interest subject to the Policy.)

During the time I am a Director or Officer of the Organization, I agree to report promptly any future direct or indirect financial, competing or other material interest or co-investment interest that is required to be disclosed under the Policy.

I am completing this disclosure statement based on the definitions below that are taken from the Conflict-of-Interest Policy.

Signature: _____ Date: _____

Please return this statement in the enclosed envelope not later than _____.

For the purposes of this Policy, a Director or Officer has a **direct or indirect financial, competing or other material interest** in a proposed or existing contract, transaction, or arrangement (collectively, "Arrangement") if he or she or one of his or her relatives

(a) has a substantial financial or competing interest directly in the proposed or existing Arrangement

(b) has a substantial financial interest in any other organization that i) is a party to the proposed or existing Arrangement, or ii) is in any way involved in the proposed or existing Arrangement, including through the provision of services in connection therewith (an "involved organization"), or iii) has a competing interest in the proposed or existing Arrangement (a "competing organization")

(c) holds a position as trustee, director, officer, member, partner, or employee in any such party to the proposed or existing Arrangement or any involved or competing organization

A Director's or Officer's financial interest will be considered substantial if it involves

(a) an ownership or investment interest representing more than 1 percent of the outstanding shares of a publicly traded company or 5 percent of the outstanding shares or comparable interest of a privately owned company with which the Organization has or is negotiating an Arrangement or which is an involved or competing organization with respect to the Arrangement

(b) an ownership or investment interest, which produces a significant amount of income for or constitutes a significant part of the net worth of the Director or Officer, or a relative of the Director or Officer, in any entity with which the Organization has or is negotiating an Arrangement or which is an involved or competing organization with respect to the Arrangement

(c) a compensation arrangement of any kind with any entity or individual with which the Organization has or is negotiating an Arrangement or with any involved or competing organization with respect to the Arrangement

Each Director and each Officer of the Organization also is required to disclose whether he or she, or one of his or her relatives, has personal funds invested with an investment manager providing, or expected to provide, investment management services to the Organization or in a professionally managed investment fund in which the Organization is invested or is considering investing (a "co-investment interest"). For the purposes of this Conflicts Policy, a "professionally managed investment fund" shall not include mutual funds or other similar investment vehicles generally available to the investing public on essentially the same terms.

APPENDIX 5

Sample Policy for the Promotion of Ethical Conduct

[Name of Organization]

POLICY FOR THE PROMOTION OF ETHICAL CONDUCT

As a nonprofit organization at the forefront of [purpose of organization], [Name]'s policy is to uphold the highest legal, ethical, and moral standards. Our donors and volunteers support [Name] because they trust us to be good stewards of their resources, and to uphold rigorous standards of conduct. Our reputation for integrity and excellence requires the careful observance of all applicable laws and regulations, as well as a scrupulous regard for the highest standards of conduct and personal integrity.

[Name] will comply with all applicable laws and regulations and expects its directors, officers, and employees to conduct business in accordance with the letter and spirit of all relevant laws; to refrain from any illegal, dishonest, or unethical conduct; to act in a professional, businesslike manner; and to treat others with respect. Directors and officers should not use their positions to obtain unreasonable or excessive services from [Name]'s staff.

In general, the use of good judgment based on high ethical principles will guide you with respect to lines of acceptable conduct. However, if a situation arises where it is difficult to determine the proper course of conduct, or where you have questions concerning the propriety of certain conduct by you or others, the matter should be brought to the attention of [Name]. If you are an employee, you should contact your immediate supervisor and, if necessary, the Director of Human Resources. Board members should raise any such concerns with the Chair or the Treasurer of [Name]'s Board.

In all questions involving ethics and conduct, the Board of Directors will make relevant determinations, except that any individual whose conduct is at issue will not participate in such decisions.

APPENDIX 6
Sample Whistleblower Policy

INTRODUCTION

The _____ (the "Organization") is committed to the highest possible legal, ethical, and moral standards of conduct and will not tolerate illegal or dishonest behavior. In this spirit, the Organization encourages employees, officers, and directors to identify any instances in which these standards may be compromised.

SCOPE

This Whistleblower Policy ("Policy") has been established to provide a means for employees, officers, and directors to raise good-faith concerns about behavior that appears to be illegal, dishonest, or unethical. A Whistleblower is the individual reporting such activity.

All employees, officers, and directors are covered under the Policy. It is the responsibility of all employees, officers, and directors to comply with the Policy and report any violations or suspected violations of the principles set forth herein.

Examples of serious misconduct covered by this Policy include, but are not limited to, violations of federal, state, or local laws; fraudulent financial reporting or actions that may lead to such fraudulent reporting; destroying, altering, concealing, or falsifying a document, or attempting to do so, with the intent to impair the document's availability for use in an official proceeding; fraudulently influencing or misleading any independent public accountant engaged in the performance of an audit of the Organization's financial statements; or planning, facilitating, or concealing any of the above.

This is not meant to be an exhaustive list but rather a guide to the types of improper behavior covered by this Policy.

Procedure for Reporting Violations

Any person may report allegations of suspected improper activities. The individuals involved in such activities may be staff, officers, directors, auditors, vendors, or other third parties.

The Organization has two Compliance Officers:_____ and _____. A Whistleblower should direct all concerns, either in written or oral form, to the Compliance Officers listed above, who will be responsible for investigating and resolving all reported complaints and allegations concerning violations of the Policy. Upon receipt of a complaint under this Policy, the Compliance Officers must advise the President or Chair of the Board. The allegation submitted by the Whistleblower should include whatever documentation is available to support a reasonable basis for the claim and to assist the Compliance Officers in investigating the allegation.

If a Whistleblower is not comfortable communicating concerns to the Compliance Officers or is unsatisfied with the response, the Whistleblower is encouraged to speak with anyone in management with whom he or she is comfortable.

Allegations may be made anonymously. Anonymous allegations should be detailed to the greatest extent possible because follow-up questions will not be possible.

Although the Whistleblower is not expected to prove the truth of the allegation(s), she or he must demonstrate reasonable grounds for concern. No investigation will be made of unspecified wrongdoing or broad allegations. The Whistleblower is not, however, responsible for investigating the activity or for determining fault or corrective measures.

Unless the allegation is submitted anonymously or there are overriding legal or public interest concerns, the Whistleblower will receive acknowledgment of receipt of the allegation within five business days. All reports will be promptly investigated and appropriate, corrective action will be taken if warranted by the investigation.

Confidentiality

Any investigation will be conducted in a manner that conceals and protects the Whistleblower's identity to the greatest extent possible, consistent with the need to conduct a fair and adequate investigation.

No Retaliation

The Organization prohibits any form of harassment, retaliation, or other adverse employment consequence toward a Whistleblower in response to a good faith allegation under this Policy. Any person who retaliates against a Whistleblower or other individual who assists in the investigation is subject to appropriate disciplinary and corrective action, up to and including termination of employment in the case of an employee.

A Whistleblower's right to protection does not extend immunity for participating or being complicit in the matters that are the subject of the allegations or ensuing investigations.

Any employee, officer or director found to have knowingly made a false allegation with malicious intent or to have knowingly produced false information with respect to the complaint will be subject to disciplinary measures.

GLOSSARY

Applicable tax-exempt organization: In the context of the intermediate sanctions rules of Internal Revenue Code Section 4958, these are Section 501(c)(3) organizations (other than private foundations) and 501(c)(4) organizations that were tax exempt at any time during a five-year period ending on the date of a transaction covered by the intermediate sanctions rules.

Arm's length transaction: This is an expression used to describe a transaction between persons in which each acts in his or her own self-interest and, except for the transaction involved, has no other relationship.

Compliance officer: An individual — board member or an independent outsider — who may be designated by an organization's board of directors to monitor disclosure statements and to serve as the point person when conflicts of interest or whistleblower complaints arise.

Conflict of interest: A situation where an officer, director, or other person with substantial influence over an organization has an existing or potential financial or other material interest that might impair his or her independence or objectivity in the discharge of responsibilities and duties to the organization.

Conflict-of-interest policy: A policy intended to protect an organization's interests when it is contemplating entering into a contract, transaction, or arrangement that might benefit the private interests of a member of the organization's board of directors, an officer of the organization, or any other individual with substantial influence over the organization. The policy is also meant to aid these individuals in performing the duties imposed upon them with respect to their management responsibilities and fiduciary obligations to the organization.

Disclosure statement: A statement on which each individual covered by an organization's conflict-of-interest policy (1) acknowledges his or her familiarity with the organization's conflict-of-interest policy and (2) discloses in writing any existing financial or other material interests or co-investment interests.

Disqualified person: In the context of the intermediate sanctions rules of Internal Revenue Code Section 4958, an individual who is in a position to exercise substantial influence over the organization at any time during a five-year period that ends on the date the transaction at issue occurred, including certain family members of such individuals, and certain 35-percent controlled entities. In the context of the private foundation rules, including the self-dealing rules, the definition is somewhat different, and includes substantial contributors to the private foundation, foundation managers, and family members of such persons (as defined under those rules).

Donor advised fund: Generally, a donor advised fund is a separately identified fund or account that may be maintained and operated by a section 501(c)(3) organization or even a for-profit investment corporation. Once the donor makes the contribution, the organization has legal control over it. However, the donor, or the donor's representative, retains advisory privileges with respect to the distribution of funds and the investment of assets in the account.

Duty of care: Requires a director or officer of a nonprofit organization to act with common sense and informed judgment and to take an active interest in the organization's activities. With respect to managing conflicts of interest, it requires the director or officer to disclose his or her material outside interests and actively participate in the managing of such interests disclosed by others. This is a legal duty explicitly recognized by virtually every state.

Duty of disclosure: The obligation imposed on the individuals covered by a conflict-of-interest policy that requires them to report to the board any actual or potential conflicts of interest.

Duty of loyalty: Requires a director or officer of a nonprofit organization to make decisions that he or she believes are in the best interests of that organization and are not designed to further his or her interests or the interests of a third party. It also requires that a board member not use his or her organizational position or knowledge to advance a personal agenda at the organization's expense or appropriate a corporate opportunity of the organization.

Duty of obedience: Requires a director or officer of a nonprofit organization to be faithful to the mission of the organization. It includes the obligation to ensure that an organization's resources are used to further the organization's mission and are not diverted to benefit private parties.

Excess benefit transaction: In the context of the intermediate sanctions rules of Internal Revenue Code Section 4958, a transaction between an organization and a disqualified person in which the value of the benefit provided by the organization to the disqualified person exceeds the value of the goods or services provided by the disqualified person in exchange for the benefit.

Fiduciary: A person standing in a special relationship of trust, confidence, or responsibility to another. Board members and officers of a nonprofit organization are fiduciaries with respect to the organization they serve and, as such, their responsibilities to the organization are termed fiduciary duties or fiduciary responsibilities.

Form 990: The IRS form titled "Return of Organization Exempt From Income Tax," that must be filed each year by exempt organizations whose annual receipts exceed a certain threshold amount. It is the main IRS reporting form for nonprofits and the principal filing with many states. An organization's Forms 990 for the past three years must be made publicly available and most Forms 990 beginning with the year 1997 are posted on the Internet. (Private foundations' returns are called Form 990-PF, Return of Private Foundation.)

Form 1023: The IRS form titled "Application for Recognition of Exemption Under Section 501(c)(3) of the Internal Revenue Code." This is the form that must be filed by organizations seeking recognition of tax exemption from the IRS as an organization described in Code Section 501(c)(3).

Independent body: A body composed entirely of individuals who do not have a conflict of interest with respect to a transaction or arrangement that is being considered by that body. This usually refers to the governing board or a committee.

Initial contract exception: In the context of the intermediate sanctions rules, there is an exception for fixed payments made pursuant to the first binding written contract (such as an employment contract) with a person who, immediately prior to entering into the contract, was not a disqualified person with respect to the organization. The exception is lost, and the contract is treated as a new contract, if the original contract is substantially modified.

Insider: For purposes of a "private inurement" analysis, an insider includes an officer, director, or founder of an organization, or a family member of any such individual, as well as certain other individuals who have a significant influence over an organization's operations.

Intermediate sanctions rules: These are the rules set forth in Internal Revenue Code Section 4958 governing transactions between certain tax-exempt organizations and disqualified persons. When an "excess benefit" transaction occurs, these rules impose penalties in the form of excise taxes on both the disqualified person who receives the excess benefit and on organization managers who participate in the approval of the transaction, knowing it to be an excess benefit transaction.

Nepotism: Favoritism shown by an individual in power to his or her relatives, particularly in hiring relatives without considering other candidates, or in providing benefits to relatives.

Private benefit doctrine: Doctrine based on the rule that exempt organizations may not benefit private persons, even though they are not "insiders," except to an insubstantial extent. With respect to the prohibition against benefiting insiders, see definition of private inurement doctrine.

Private foundation: Generally, a private foundation is a tax-exempt charitable organization that is initially funded from one source (usually an individual, a married couple, a family, or a business) and that makes grants for charitable purposes.

Private inurement doctrine: The prohibition on certain tax-exempt organizations transferring any funds to insiders as if they were owners, whether through excessive compensation, by overpaying for goods or services, or otherwise.

Public charity: A nonprofit organization that is exempt from federal income tax under Internal Revenue Code Section 501(c)(3) and that is not a private foundation. Certain religious, educational, and health care institutions are deemed to be public charities by virtue of what they do. Other exempt organizations wishing to be considered public charities must either pass a public support test demonstrating broad financial support or must be formed to benefit an organization that is a public charity.

Publicly supported organization: A nonprofit organization that is exempt from federal income tax under Internal Revenue Code Section 501(c)(3) and that has passed one of the public support tests contained in Internal Revenue Code Section 509(a). As indicated above, a publicly supported organization is one type of public charity.

Reasonable compensation: Generally, compensation paid for services actually rendered in such amount as ordinarily would be paid for like services by like enterprises under similar circumstances.

Rebuttable presumption of reasonableness: A safe harbor under Internal Revenue Code Section 4958 setting forth steps that must be taken with respect to a transaction between a disqualified person and an applicable tax-exempt organization to (i) create a presumption that the transaction's terms are "reasonable," and (ii) shift the burden to the IRS to prove that the terms are not reasonable.

Sarbanes-Oxley Act of 2002: Sarbanes-Oxley was enacted by Congress in response to the wave of corporate scandals that included Enron and WorldCom. The goal of Sarbanes-Oxley is to protect the interests of shareholders and the public by preventing fraudulent practices and accounting inconsistencies. The Act focuses on the integrity of financial information, the adequacy of internal financial controls, and the independence of auditors. Except for certain provisions on whistleblowing and record retention, it does not apply to nonprofit organizations.

Self-dealing: Financial transactions and arrangements between a private foundation and a disqualified person (as that term is defined in the private foundation rules) that are strictly prohibited under Internal Revenue Code Section 4941, regardless of whether the transaction is a fair-market-value transaction, or even results in a benefit to the private foundation. Self-dealing acts include (with certain exceptions) property transactions, loans, and furnishing of goods, services, or facilities.

Social-welfare organization: An organization described in Internal Revenue Code Section 501(c)(4) and operated primarily to further the common good and general welfare of the people of a community, such as by bringing about civic betterment and social improvements. These organizations are not subject to the limitations on legislative lobbying imposed on Section 501(c)(3) organizations.

Supporting organization: A supporting organization is a 501(c)(3) organization that carries out its exempt purposes by supporting other exempt organizations, usually other public charities and derives it public charity status by virtue of its relationship with one or more other public charities. Supporting organizations are classified under Section 509(a)(3) of the Code.

Tax-exempt organization: An organization exempt from federal income tax under Internal Revenue Code Section 501(a). There are 29 different types of tax-exempt organizations listed under Code Section 501(c), but, of these, Section 501(c)(3) organizations are the only ones to which tax-deductible contributions may be made, with the exception of certain types of contributions to certain veterans organizations, fraternal societies, and cemetery companies.

Transparency: A continuous flow of information from an organization to the public about the organization's mission, financial situation, and governance practices.

SUGGESTED RESOURCES

BoardSource. *The Nonprofit Board Answer Book: Practical Guidelines for Board Members and Chief Executives, Third Edition*. San Francisco: Jossey-Bass, 2012. Our revised edition of this best-selling book is organized into 85 easy-to-follow questions-and-answers and covers almost every situation you're likely to encounter in nonprofit board governance, from structuring a board for success to nurturing strategic alliances with other organizations. Also included are action steps, real-life examples, and worksheets.

BoardSource. *The Source: Twelve Principles of Governance That Power Exceptional Boards*. Washington, DC: BoardSource, 2005. Exceptional boards add significant value to their organizations, making discernible differences in their advance on mission. Such boards define governance not as dry, obligatory compliance but as a creative and collaborative process that supports chief executives, engages board members, and furthers the causes they all serve. This book helps nonprofit boards operate at the highest level of their collective capacity. Aspirational in nature, these principles offer chief executives a description of an empowered board that is a strategic asset to be leveraged, and they provide board members with a vision of what is possible and a way to add lasting value to the organizations they lead.

Flynn, Outi. *Meeting, and Exceeding Expectations: A Guide to Successful Nonprofit Board Meetings, Second Edition*. Washington, DC: BoardSource, 2009. This book provides information that will help your board have more productive meetings. This resource poses critical questions, provides easy-to-implement answers, suggests tools, clarifies legal and ethical expectations, and suggests ways to handle conflicts of interest that arise during meetings. Nine appendices provide sample meeting agendas, minutes templates, contents of a board book, and more.

Hopkins, Bruce R. *Legal Responsibilities of Nonprofit Boards, Second Edition*. Washington, DC: BoardSource, 2009. All board members should understand their legal responsibilities, including when and how they can be held personally liable and what type of oversight they should provide. Discover the essential information that board members should know to protect themselves and their organization. Written in nontechnical language, this book provides legal concepts and definitions, as well as a detailed discussion on ethics.

Lakey, Berit M. *Board Fundamentals: Understanding Roles in Nonprofit Governance, Second Edition*. Washington, DC: BoardSource, 2010. This book outlines the essentials of nonprofit governance and describes ways that boards and board members can add value to the organizations they serve. It defines the difference between policy making and management and outlines the basic responsibilities of a nonprofit board, including setting organizational direction, ensuring necessary resources, and providing oversight.

Lawrence, Barbara and Outi Flynn. *The Nonprofit Policy Sampler, Second Edition*. Washington, DC: BoardSource, 2006. In addition to steering an organization's activities, nonprofit boards are also responsible for setting policies that govern their own actions. This resource provides nonprofit leaders with more than 200 sample board policies and job descriptions collected from a wide variety of nonprofits. The user's guide provides a basic overview of each of the policies, which may be easily customized to suit your organization.

Tesdahl, D. Benson. *Better Bylaws: Creating Effective Rules for Your Nonprofit Board, Second Edition*. Washington, DC: BoardSource, 2010. It is important that your board periodically review and adjust its bylaws in response to organizational change and growth. This revised book will help your board determine the best structure for your organization, the rights of the participants within the structure, and important board procedures. Sample bylaws provisions and conflicts-of-interest policies are included.

Vogel, Brian H. and Charles W. Quatt. *Nonprofit Executive Compensation: Planning, Performance, and Pay, Second Edition*. Washington, DC: BoardSource, 2010. This resource explains how nonprofits of all types can increase the transparency and integrity of chief executive compensation practices as part of their stewardship of the public trust. As the authors examine important parts of the process such as board responsibilities, chief executive assessment, contracts, IRS regulations, legal standards, and compensation packages, they guide nonprofit boards through the process of setting an effective chief executive compensation plan.

Wertheimer, Mindy R., PhD. *The Board Chair Handbook, Third Edition*. Washington, DC: BoardSource, 2013. Whether you are a seasoned board chair, an incoming chair, or considering the position, this guide provides the blueprint for the position and the responsibilities that come with it. It focuses on the chair's leadership role on the board, addresses the partnership with the chief executive, and outlines the communication skills required. Sample agendas and letters are included.

ABOUT THE AUTHORS

Sarah E. Paul is of counsel at Skadden, Arps, Slate, Meagher & Flom LLP and is deputy head of the exempt organizations practice. She has specialized in representing tax-exempt organizations for nearly 25 years, both in private practice and, early in her career, as the deputy counsel of The New York Public Library. Ms. Paul has particular expertise on corporate governance issues and on the tax laws relating to tax-exempt organizations of all types. She has served on the boards of James Lenox House Association, which provides secure and affordable living for elderly persons with limited financial resources, and Pro Mujer (Programs for Women), a women's development organization that uses microlending, business training, and health care support to help women improve their lives and those of their families.

Ms. Paul graduated summa cum laude and Phi Beta Kappa from Harvard College and earned her law degree cum laude from Harvard Law School.

Daniel L. Kurtz, a lawyer for more than 40 years, heads Skadden, Arps, Slate, Meagher & Flom LLP's national practice on exempt organizations. A leading expert on nonprofit governance, he has written extensively in the field, including legal treatises and publications for lay audiences. He served as assistant attorney general-in-charge of the New York State Attorney General's Charities Bureau for six years in the 1980s and has devoted the last 25 years, since leaving government service, to his private practice representing exclusively tax-exempt organizations.

Mr. Kurtz has led an active volunteer life, serving on the boards of numerous nonprofit organizations, including Jewish Home and Hospital for the Aged, one of the nation's leading voluntary nursing homes, and Fountain House, a highly regarded agency providing a broad range of services to the mentally ill. He is currently a member of the board of overseers of Bard College at Simon's Rock, president of Manhattan Youth Recreation and Resources, president of The Spingold Foundation, and a board member of two other family foundations. He has been active in and chaired committees dealing with nonprofit issues for legal professional associations at the national, state, and local levels. Mr. Kurtz is a graduate of Brown University and the University of Chicago Law School.